Camera Work

Camera Work

Stieglitz, Steichen
and their Contemporaries

Introduction and Notes
by Françoise Heilbrun

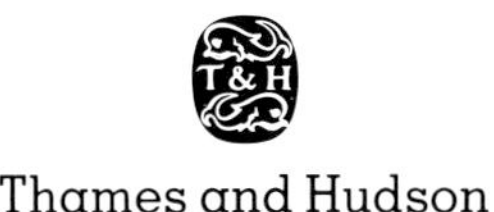

Thames and Hudson

Translated from the French by Ruth Sharman

On the cover: Edward J. Steichen, *Steeplechase Day, Paris; After the Races*, 1913

First published in Great Britain in 1991 by
Thames and Hudson Ltd, London
Originally published in France by the Centre National de la Photographie

Printed and bound in Italy

CAMERA WORK
DEFENCE AND ILLUSTRATION OF
PICTORIALIST PHOTOGRAPHY

At the turn of the century, following the appearance of portable snapshot cameras of the Kodak type (c. 1887), photography became easy to practise and accessible to virtually anybody; it was no longer simply a craft reserved for professionals or an elite group. Thanks to the ease with which the new cameras could be handled and the increased sensitivity of the emulsions, the expressive possibilities of the medium were considerably enhanced. And since photography had now matured technically and its processes were no longer surrounded by an aura of magic, attention began to shift quite naturally to content rather than technique, in other words, to the photographic vision. The time had come for photography to be considered as a serious art form, and the increasingly broad public to which it was being introduced would henceforth add new weight to the concerns of a handful of amateurs.

In the artistic field, this was a time of great moment for these 'amateurs': abandoning the academies and grouped in free associations, from now on they alone would be responsible for bringing about a renaissance parallel to that heralded by William Morris in the decorative arts. In the manner of painters, sculptors and architects, these photographers created their own clubs, whose aim, in defending artistic photography, was to pick up from where the existing official institutions left off. These official institutions, like London's Royal Photographic Society or Paris's Société Française de Photographie, had become the refuge not only of men of science but of commercial photographers too, since to join them required no more than payment of the subscription fee.

From among the ranks of the amateur photographers, one man in particular stands out: the Englishman Peter Henry Emerson, who gave up a promising career in medicine in the 1880s in order to indulge his passion for photography, and who has come to be regarded as the true father of 'pictorialism', a photographer who succeeded in affirming the status of his craft as a medium of original artistic expression. For Emerson, a great admirer of Jean-François Millet and the Impressionists, the true aim of art was to reproduce nature and reality, not as they actually were, but as perceived by the human eye; and photography, in spite of the absence of colour, was in Emerson's view the most appropriate means for translating these appearances – more appropriate even than painting, thanks to the extraordinarily rich tonal range it permitted. We may smile today at Emerson's laborious attempts to prove scientifically that the photographer's vision corresponds most closely to the vision of the human eye, but he was perfectly justified in insisting that photography could be something quite different from the mechanical, non-selective imitation of reality (he was later to retract this opinion) to which its detractors sought to reduce it. Unlike Oscar Gustav Rejlander or Henry Peach Robinson, however, with their fastidious reconstructions of photographed paintings, Emerson avoided aping academic painting in an endeavour to elevate photography to the level of art. His photographs of working people and marshlands in East Anglia include a number of masterpieces which, without being slavish imitations, in their own way rival the paintings of his models, Millet and Monet.

An uncompromising person, indifferent to public acclaim, Emerson had no hand in officially establishing the movement to which he had given the initial impetus (its name was adumbrated in the title of a paper he gave: 'Photography, a Pictorial Art?'), but he found an heir – one he more or less acknowledged – in the person of Alfred Stieglitz. Stieglitz was the driving force behind the New York group Photo-Secession, whose magazine, *Camera Work* (1903–17), provides a striking illustration of that early struggle to achieve recognition for photography as an art form in its own right.

The son of a wealthy industrialist of German extraction who had settled in New Jersey, Stieglitz was, like Emerson, the very embodiment of the amateur in the best sense of the word. After receiving an education in Germany, where he studied chemistry under Hermann Wilhelm Vogel, in 1883 he resolved to devote his life to photography. By taking over the management of a printing works, on his return to the United States in 1891, he was engaging in the best possible training for his future activities: *Camera Work* was in fact the third photography magazine he edited. Since 1855, the perfecting of photomechanical reproduction methods, such as photogravure, which produced a faithful equivalent of the original image while ensuring its permanence and the potential for multiple copies, had armed the defenders of artistic photography with valuable encouragement, as had the marketing of a variety of beautiful paper, including the platinum paper which Emerson was one of the first to use, and the development of sophisticated techniques of the gum bichromate type.

The photographers who grouped themselves around Stieglitz, all of them American and all amateurs, came for the most part from fairly humble backgrounds: Clarence H. White was the son of a travelling salesman in Newark, Edward J. Steichen was the son of a miner, and both were obliged to earn a living from their photography. White gave up his job as a bookseller in order to become a travelling photographer and Steichen opened a portrait studio. What remained paramount for both of them was to continue to approach their work as artists practising within the framework of the Photo-Secession group. This was a rule of thumb and determined the choice of subject matter destined either for publication (in *Camera Work* or any other magazine) or for exhibition purposes (in galleries or the numerous international photographic shows).

The Photo-Secessionists were not engaged in reportage or any activity that could be described as documentary. Alfred Stieglitz and Alvin Langdon Coburn's views of Paris, London and New York, and even Frederick H. Evans's cathedrals, are impressions or symbolic evocations translating a personal vision. And the portraits, to the extent that the model was chosen by the artist himself (generally among his acquaintance), are freely interpreted according to personal convictions, rather than designed to appeal to an anonymous clientele. In this field, Steichen was able to exert sufficient authority to impose his own style, even when dealing with a commissioned portrait. He was an exception, however, and in the long run this free scope to the photographers' imagination, this absence of exterior constraints such as a commission imposed, proved paralysing for a number of pictorialists of less individualistic bent.

Over and beyond their indisputable artistic aspirations, the fact that these photographers were self-trained ensured a common bond: it provided them with an enthusiasm and a boldness of approach that guaranteed their success as a group. Edward Steichen had followed in a Milwaukee daily the scandal caused by the unveiling of Auguste Rodin's *Balzac* in Paris. He regarded this statue – which was later to be the subject of three masterful photographs, taken by Steichen in moonlight – as the finest expression of human genius. It was in order to meet Rodin, Monet and other artists, and to photograph them, that in 1900 Steichen decided to spend a year living in Paris and travelling in Europe; at that stage in his career he was still hesitating between painting and photography. By the time he returned to the United States he had decided definitively in favour of photography; in the meantime he had also become acquainted with, among others, Rodin, Maeterlinck and George Bernard Shaw, and had familiarized himself with contemporary art in Europe, where he returned at regular intervals in the years to come. Thanks to him, the Photo-Secession group's Little Gallery, which was initially devoted exclusively to photographic exhibitions, began in 1908 introducing the American public to the work of Toulouse-Lautrec, Van Gogh, Cézanne and Matisse, and later to that of Picasso and Picabia. Quite spontaneously, one might almost say playfully, the members of the group had succeeded in maintaining that harmonious balance between their respective passions for photography and the major arts which the European pictorialists, and in particular the French, had sought in vain to achieve.

The Photo-Secessionists viewed this relationship as one of equality and of emulation, but not of subservience; thus, the example of Cubism encouraged certain American pictorialists such as Stieglitz, Steichen, Paul Strand and Adolf de Meyer to adopt a fresh starting point by ridding themselves of pictorialist sentimentalism and soft-focus effects. It was characteristic of the group that Stieglitz, while continuing to ask painters to collaborate on *Camera Work* and to proffer their opinions on the magazine, had quickly abandoned the idea of inviting painters and sculptors to act as judges at photographic shows – a custom established by the European pictorialists – since in his view photographers continued to be the best judges of their own art. And it was clear that the two pillars of the magazine, Sadakichi Hartman (alias Sidney Allan) and Charles Caffin, who started out as art critics, had selected photography as the principal, if not the exclusive, area of their investigations.

The energy of the American pictorialists is no doubt due to the sense they had of contributing to the creation of a national art, on an equal footing with the painters and sculptors they felt qualified to rival. In Europe, on the other hand, the crushing weight of a rich and living artistic tradition undoubtedly paralysed the pictorialists, to the extent that they could not endeavour to challenge the artists on their own ground. Steichen's almost obsessional taste for night scenes and mist-laden forests, and Gertrude Käsebier or Clarence White's predilection for intimate family or, by contrast, vaguely mythological scenes, show how heavily they too were influenced by Impressionism and Symbolism. But in their work such an influence was liberating rather than constraining, and, overall, they approached these themes with the same conviction and the same freshness as if they had been the first to do so. When confronted with a landscape, a dancer, or a little girl, a photographer like Robert Demachy, on the other hand, did not always succeed in forgetting Degas or Renoir, whose work he often did no more than imitate.

One of the most hotly contested issues that *Camera Work* reflected – an issue which continues to be relevant today – concerned the degree of acceptable intervention by the photographer, either while taking his photograph or during the printing of it. Was this intervention itself not precisely a guarantee of the artistic status of the photograph? Although an exponent of a kind of naturalism very close to Emerson's, Stieglitz had the good sense to display far greater openness than his predecessor and to allow *Camera Work* to become a forum for the most widely divergent opinions. Thus, one question raised was whether an element of fiction could be introduced into photography as it could into painting. Whereas many pictorialists were only too eager to people their compositions with nymphs, genies and mythological or even religious figures, the strictest purists, like de Meyer or Evans, rejected such artifice.

With regard to the role that the artist's hand could play in the interpretation itself of the subject, the group was once more divided into two opposing camps: those who preached purity of technique (Stieglitz, Evans, White, de Meyer), for whom the only justifiable manipulation could be a chemical (during development and printing), or, at most, a manual one, in order to correct a fault – on condition that such manipulation remained invisible – and those, on the other hand, who regarded manipulation as an acceptable part of the artistic process. Of the latter, Steichen favoured complex processes while continuing to respect the essentially photographic nature of the print, whereas Frank Eugene or James Craig Annan went so far as to scratch their negatives in order to give the image the appearance of a dry-point etching, and Constant Puyo, Robert Demachy, Heinrich Kuehn and others not only systematically enlarged details of their prints but increased their pictorialism by subjecting them, sometimes repeatedly, to the gum bichromate process. This technique had been developed by a certain Rouillé-Ladévèze from Alphonse Louis Poitevin's carbon process, invented in 1855. The basic principle, which opened the way for any number of new combinations, consisted in coating the support paper, using a brush, with an organic substance such as carbon or any other pigment which, when mixed with ammonium or potassium bichromate, hardened on exposure to light.

By adding brush strokes and exploiting the graininess of the pigment material, the photographer could variously reinforce such pictorial effects as he had already obtained by the use of colour. For Robert Demachy, a peerless technician who ensured the spread of this method throughout Europe and the United States, the technique was a means to a more precise rendering of tonal values, thereby perfecting without distorting the photographic vision. Like Demachy, the French pictorialists had a tendency to favour technique to the detriment of expression, and many of them gave up their photographic activities at the onset of the 1914 war, which deprived them not only of leisure time but also of the materials indispensable to their photographic concoctions. The most skilled of the Photo-Secessionists, on the other hand, discovered means of adapting to techniques and to fresh ways of thinking: for them, pictorialism was simply the springboard from which they plunged into a long and fruitful career. The pictorialists had unanimously rejected unadorned reality, viewing it as unartistic. Such an aversion expressed itself in technical terms by a softening of focus, the merits of which Steichen claimed to have discovered in a highly experimental fashion when he allowed his viewfinder to become misted over with dew. A soft-focus effect could be obtained by giving the camera a jolt just as the picture was being taken; and the graininess of the pigment in the gum bichromate mixture also contributed to a lack of definition.

With his famous photograph *The Steerage* (1907), which reproduced, this time in rather sharp focus, a wretchedly overcrowded ship's deck, Stieglitz appeared to have regained that direct handle on reality and that immediacy of feel which had characterized the very first works in the photographic medium and which continued to be the mark of a handful of truly great professionals, like Jacob Riis, Lewis Hine and Atget, who skirted the fringes of pictorialism.

The lesson taught by pictorialism – which the Bauhaus photographers and the photographers of the Russian Revolution would turn to account a decade later – was perhaps ultimately that creative photography would suffer a similar impoverishment whether it cut itself off totally from other aspects (scientific, commercial and documentary) of the medium or whether it forged overly close links with them. Pictorialism represents an important landmark in the history of photography, nevertheless: it embraced, sometimes with clumsy enthusiasm, the primacy of the photographer's personal vision, while at the same time emphasizing a contradictory but significant aspect of photography: the role of imagination.

Françoise Heilbrun

1. Edward J. Steichen,
Portraits – Evening, 1906

*The dates given are those of
publication of the photographs in
Camera Work.*

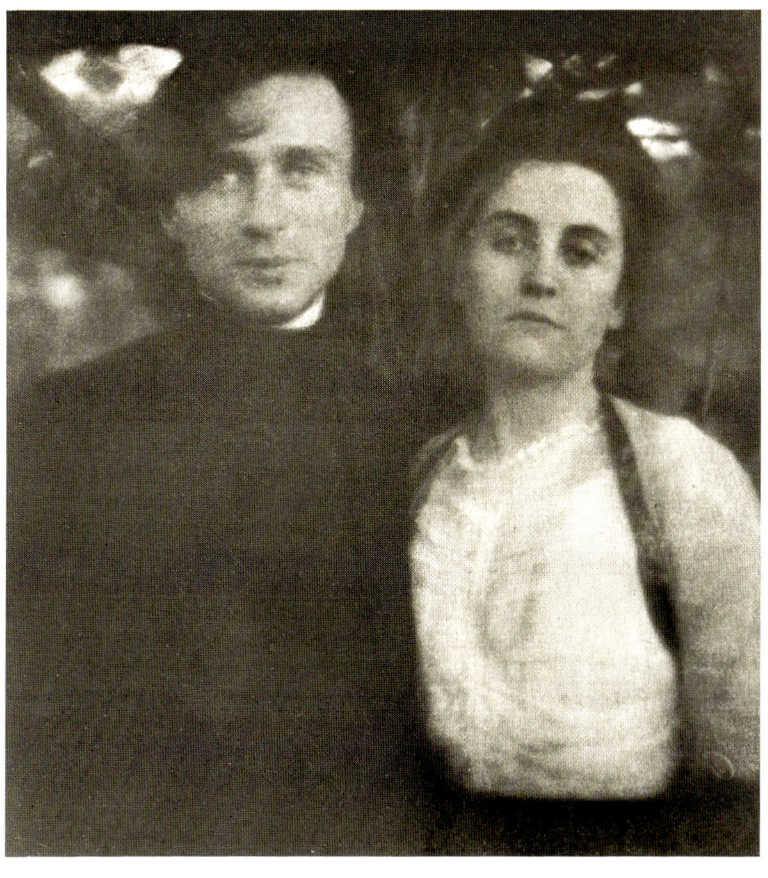

2. Edward J. Steichen,
Moonlight: The Pond, 1906

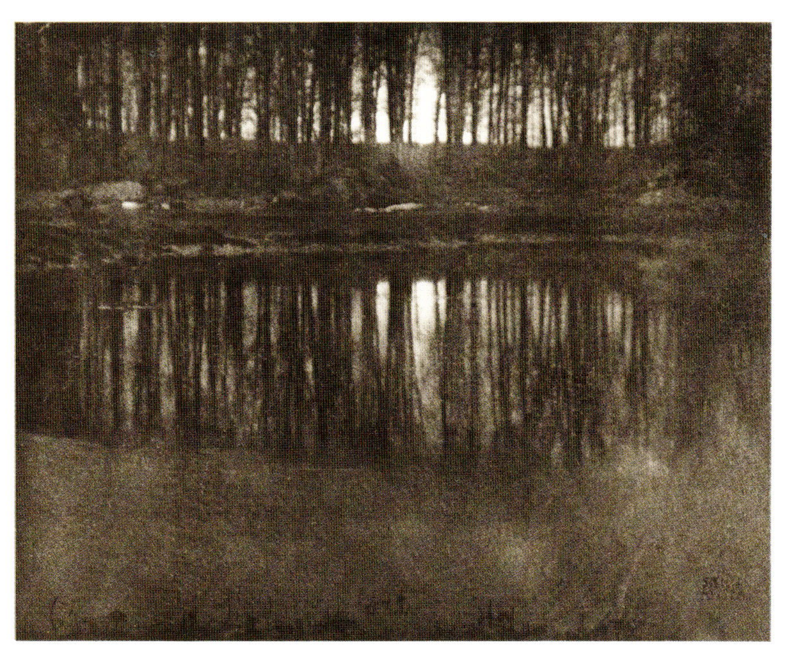

3. Edward J. Steichen,
The Pool, 1903

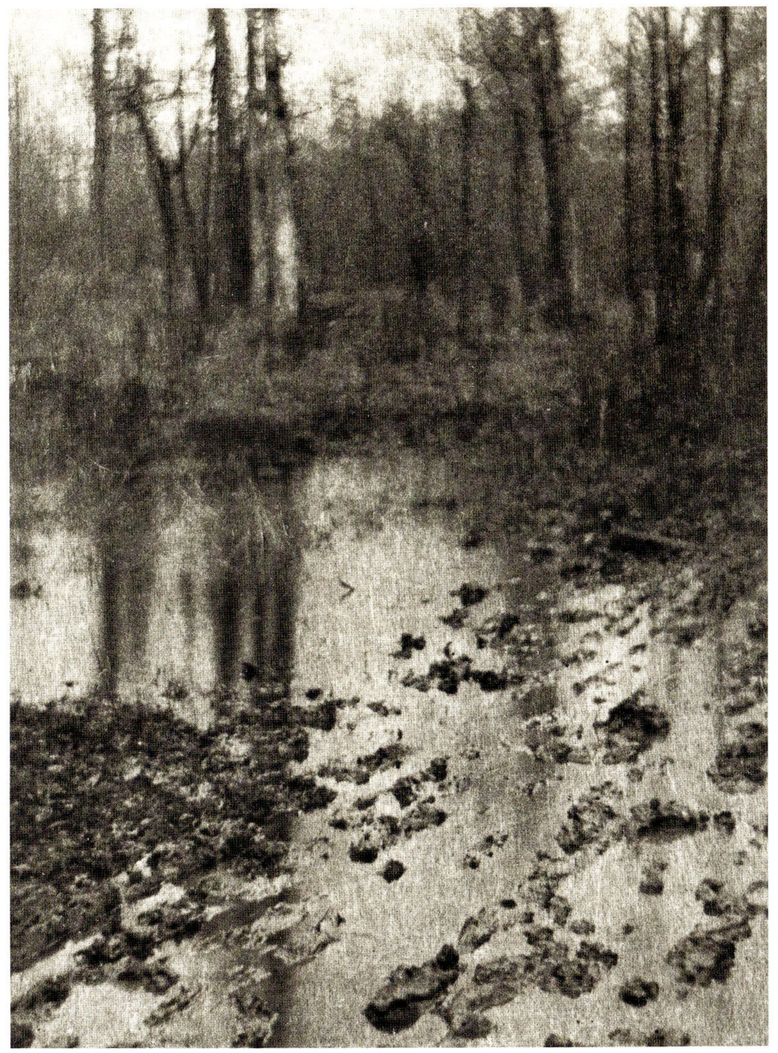

4. Edward J. Steichen,
Pastoral – Moonlight, 1907

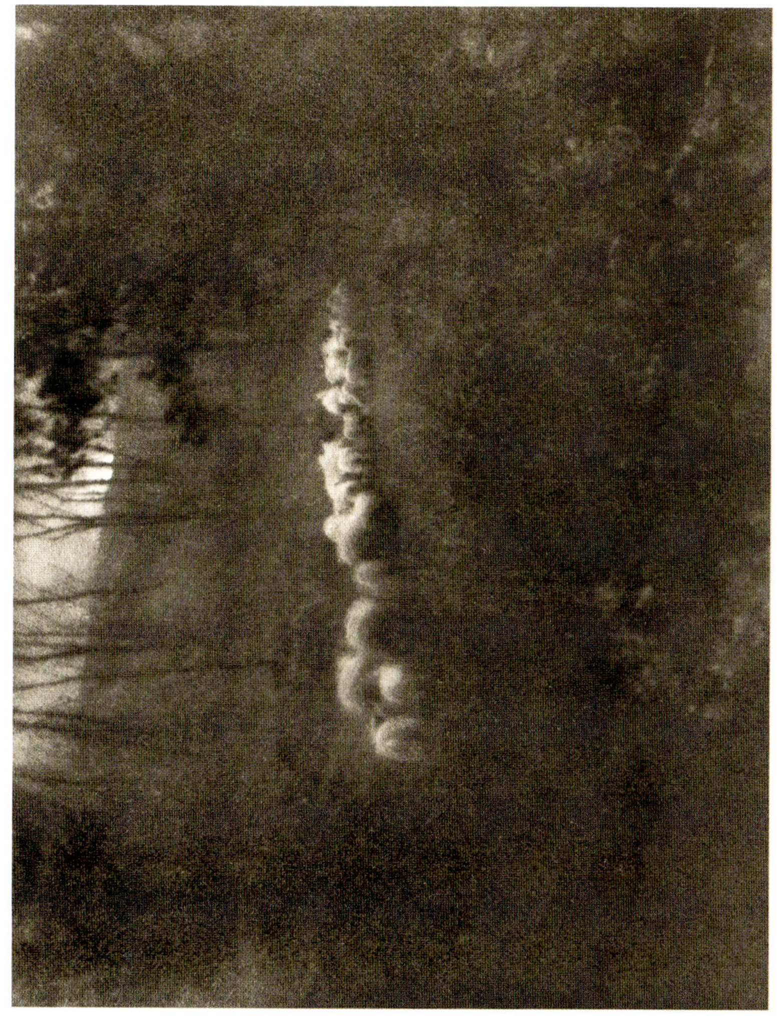

5. Clarence H. White,
Portrait – Master Tom, 1908

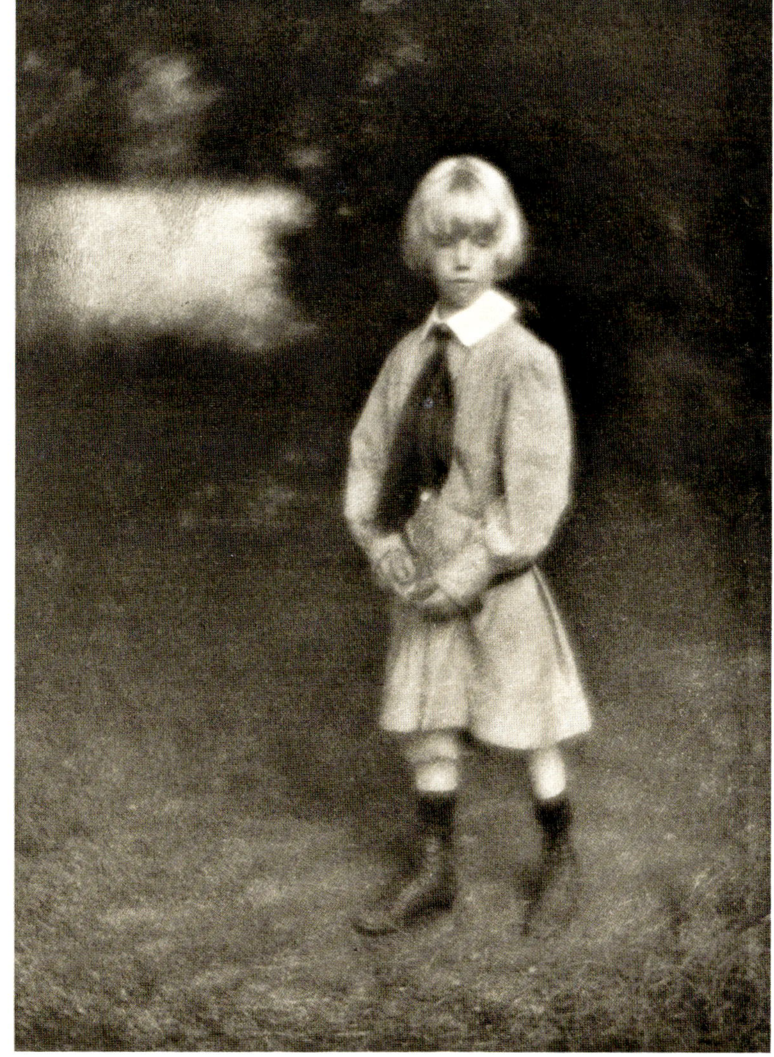

6. Edward J. Steichen,
The Big White Cloud, 1906

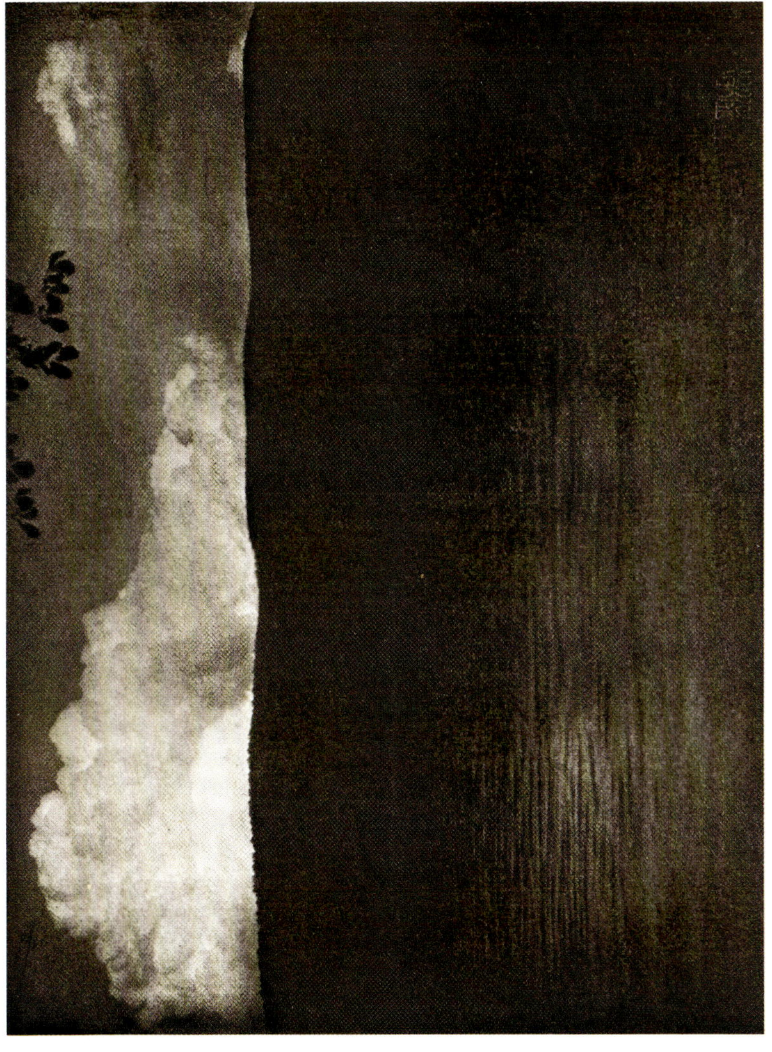

7. Heinrich Kuehn,
Lotte and Her Nurse, 1911

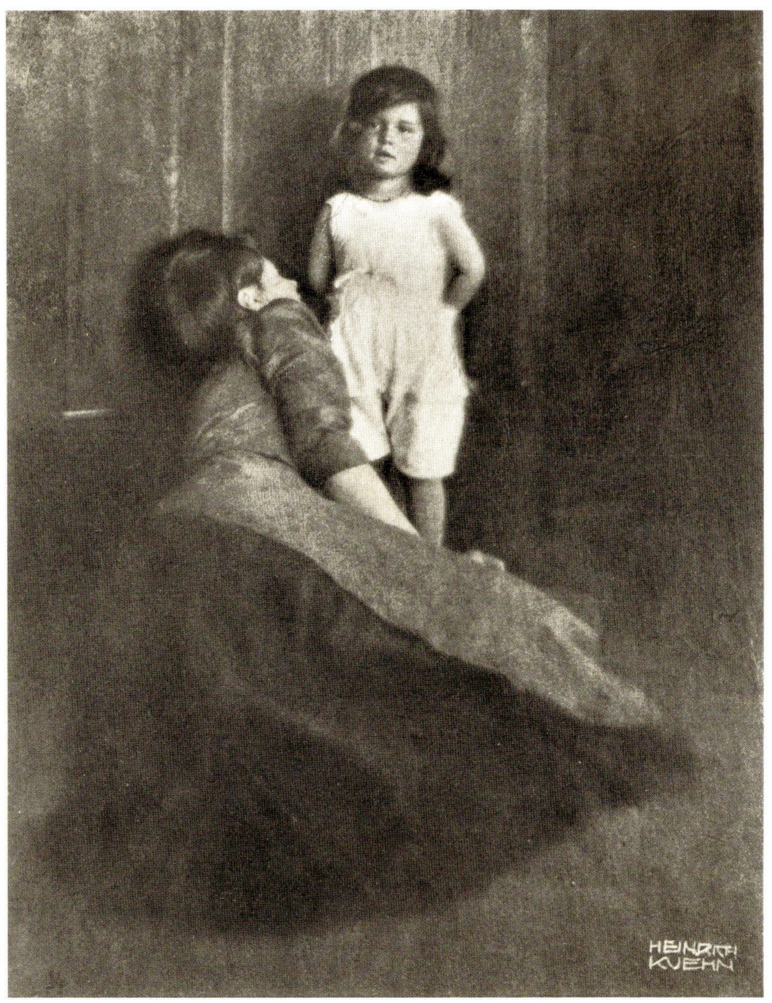

8. Adolf de Meyer,
Still Life, 1908

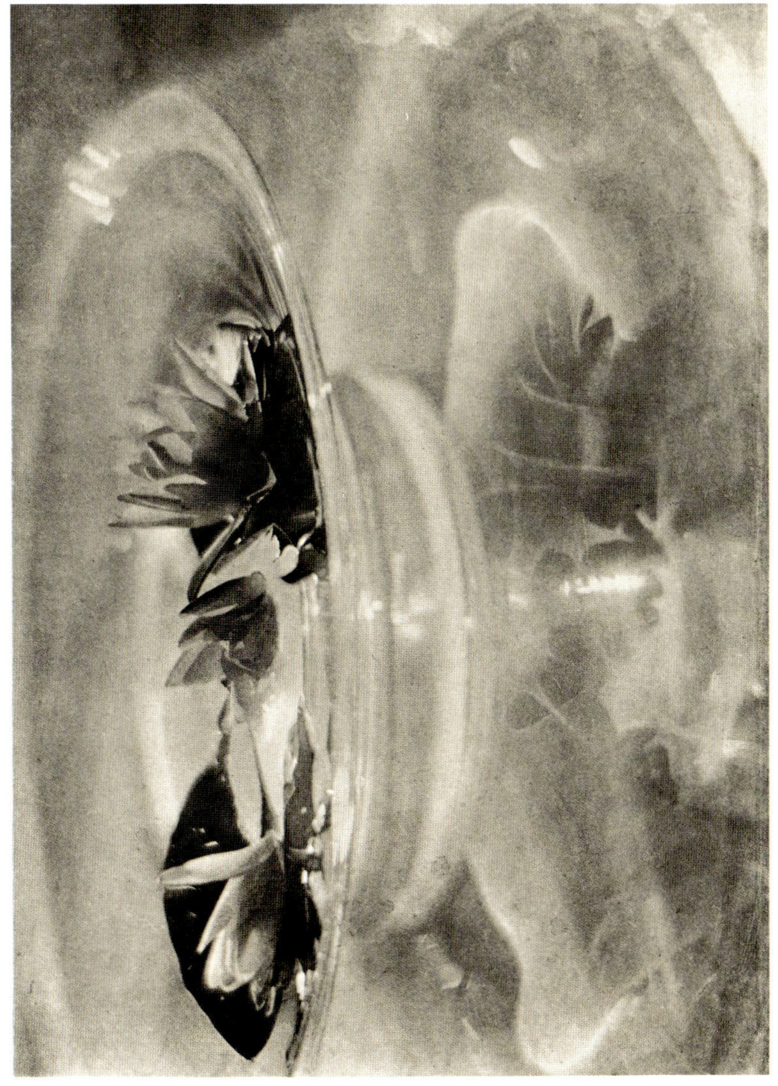

9. Clarence H. White,
Ring Toss, 1903

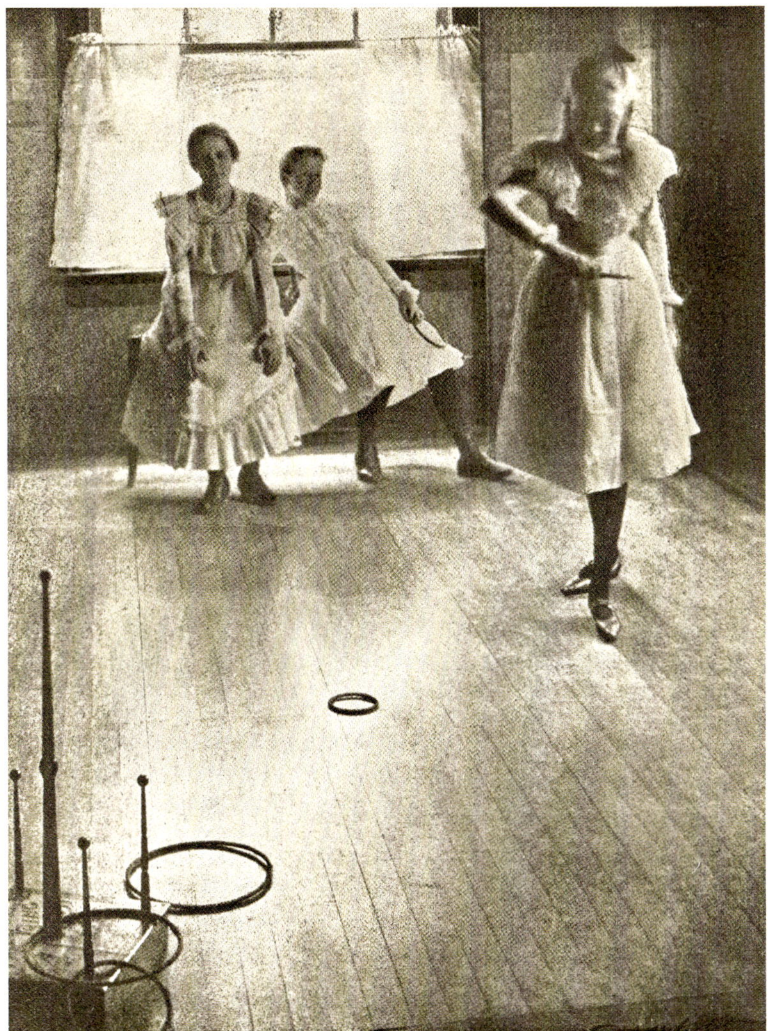

10. Joseph T. Keiley,
A Garden of Dreams, 1907

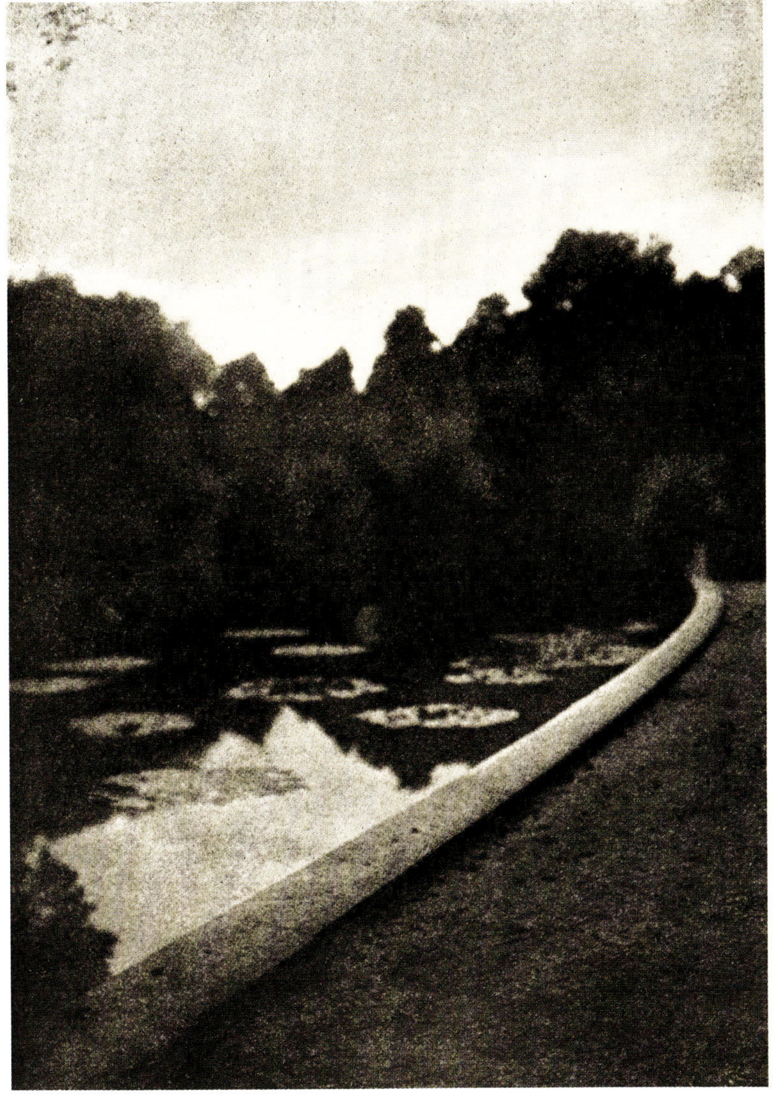

11. Edward J. Steichen,
Solitude, 1906

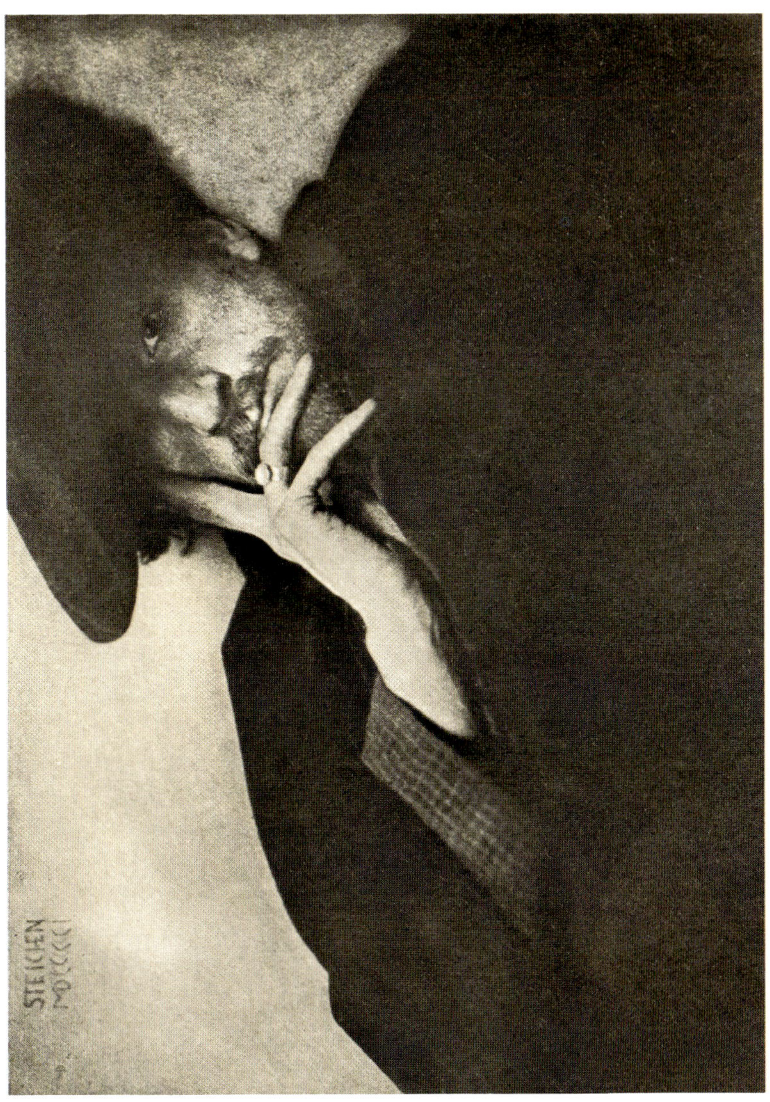
STEICHEN
MDCCCCI

12. Robert Demachy,
Speed, 1904

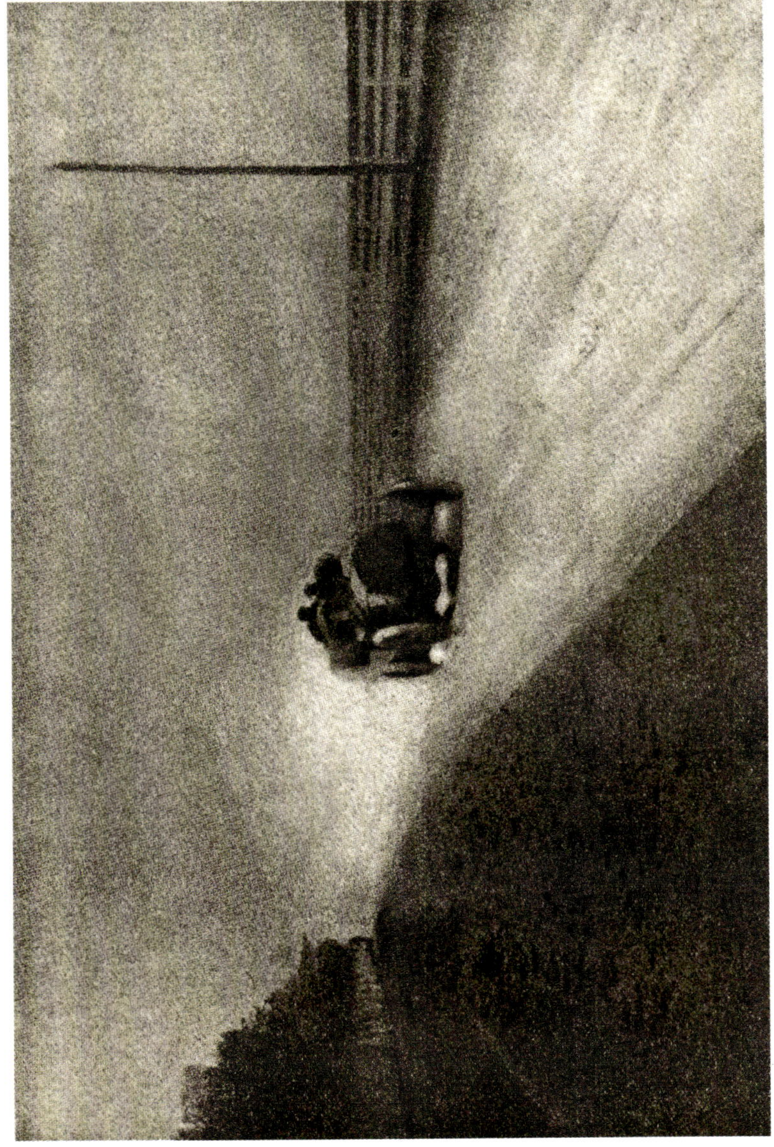

13. Alvin Langdon Coburn,
The Bridge – Ipswich, 1904

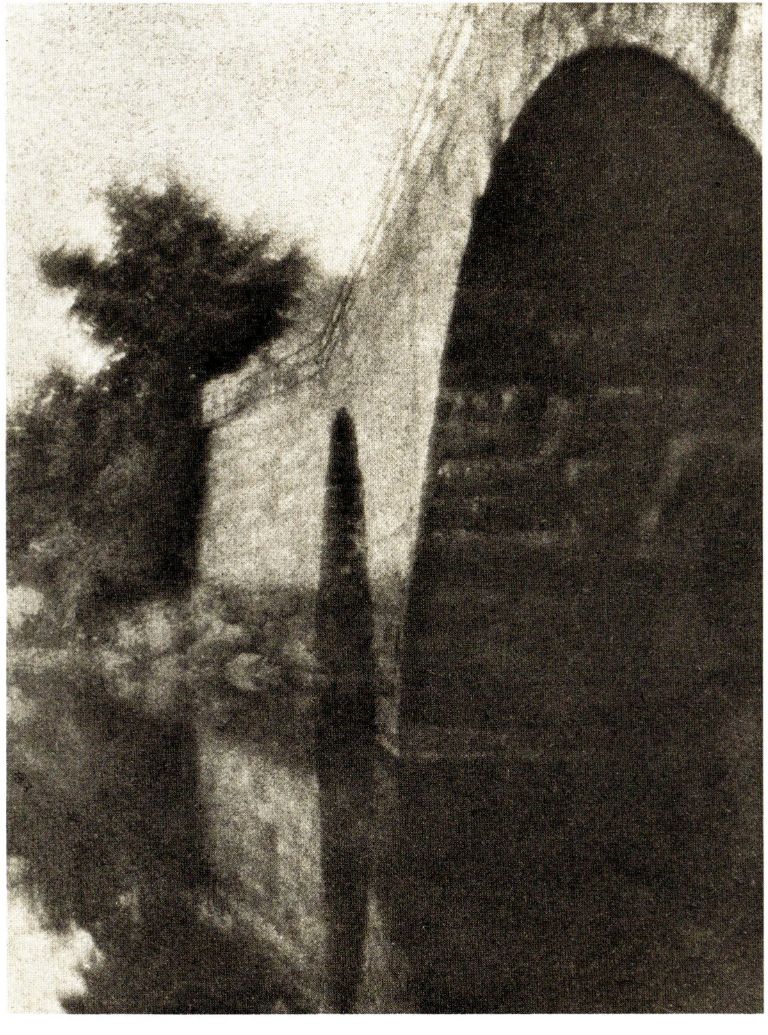

14. Edward J. Steichen,
Self-portrait, 1903

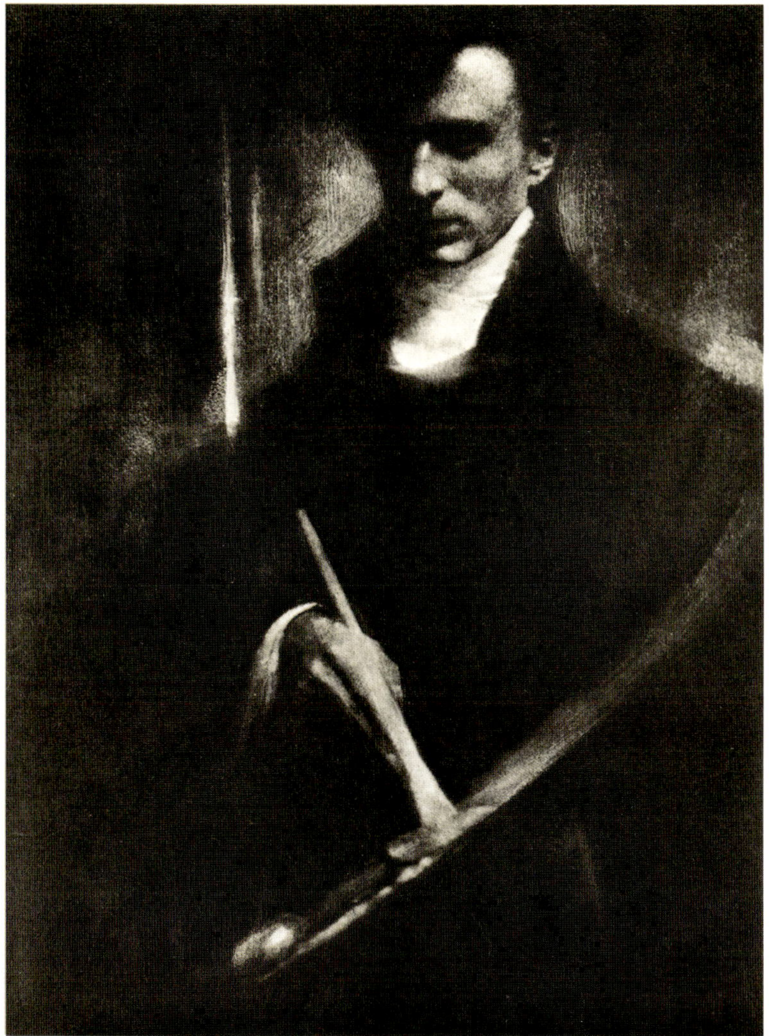

15. Edward J. Steichen,
La Cigale, 1906

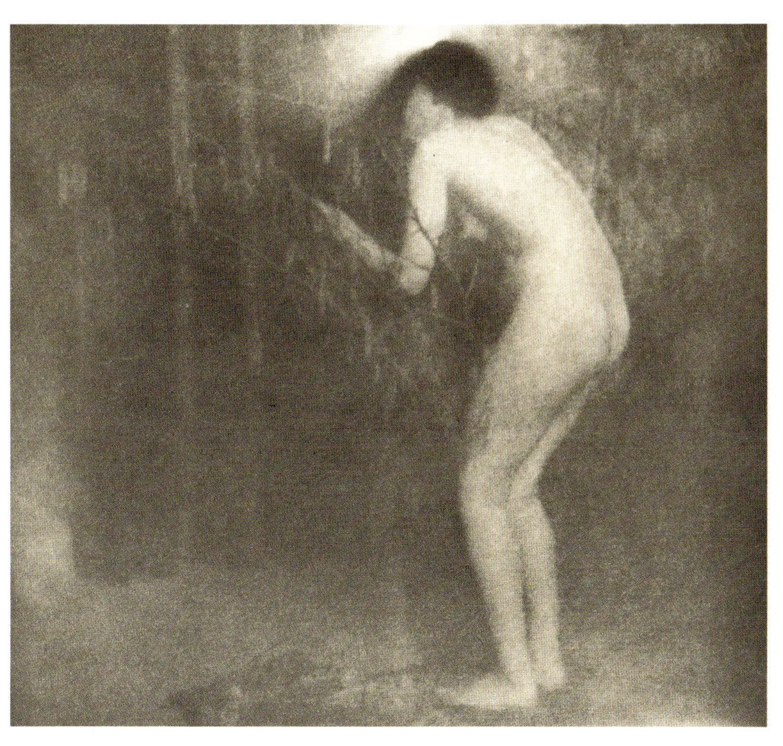

16. Robert Demachy,
Contrasts, 1904

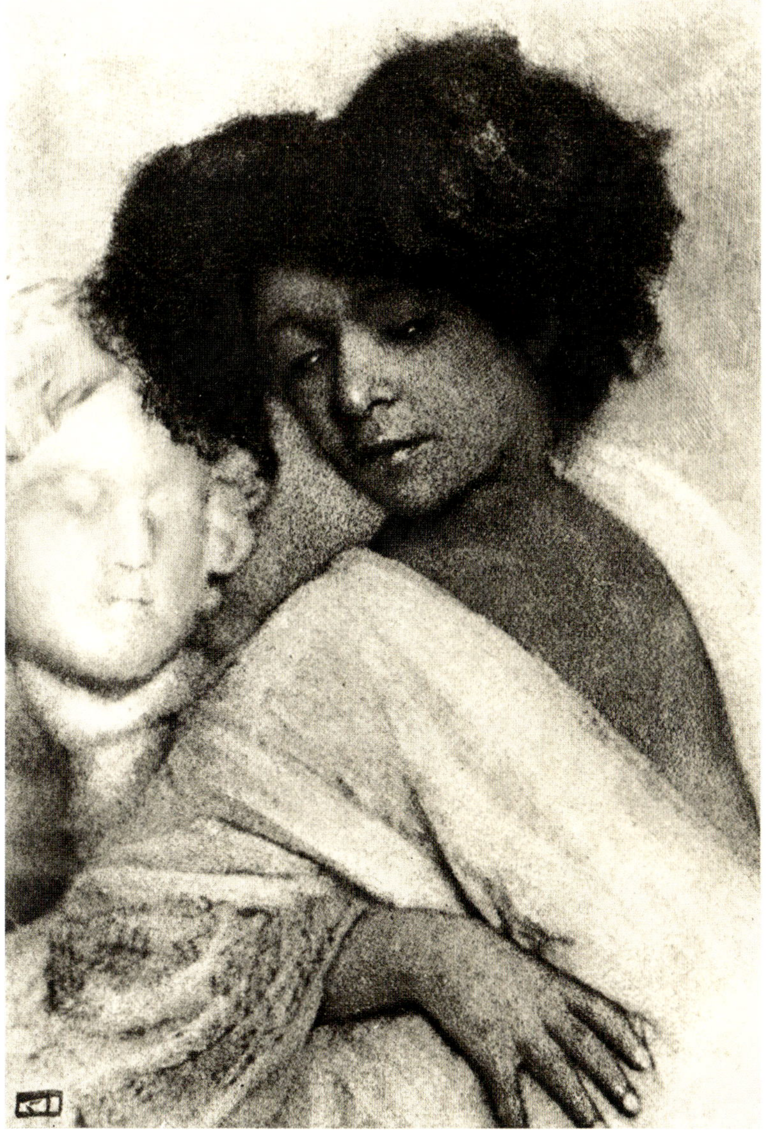

17. Robert Demachy,
Struggle, 1904

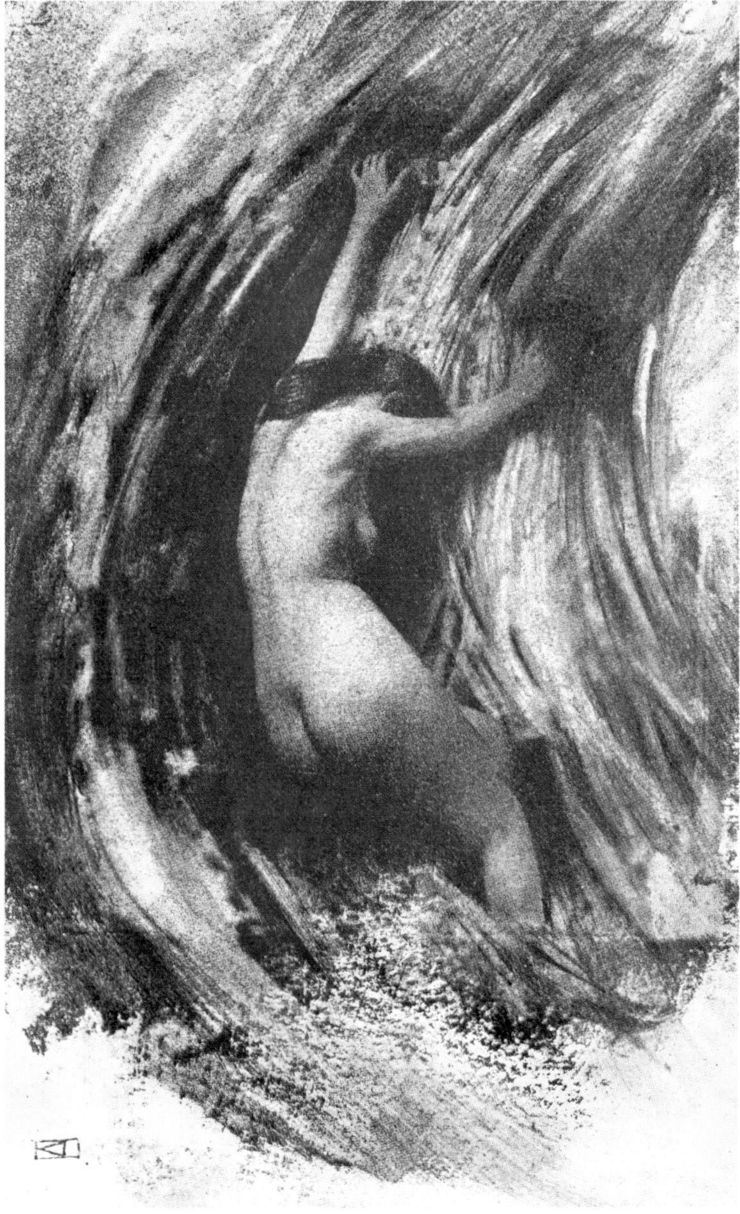

18. Edward J. Steichen,
Portrait of Clarence H. White, 1905

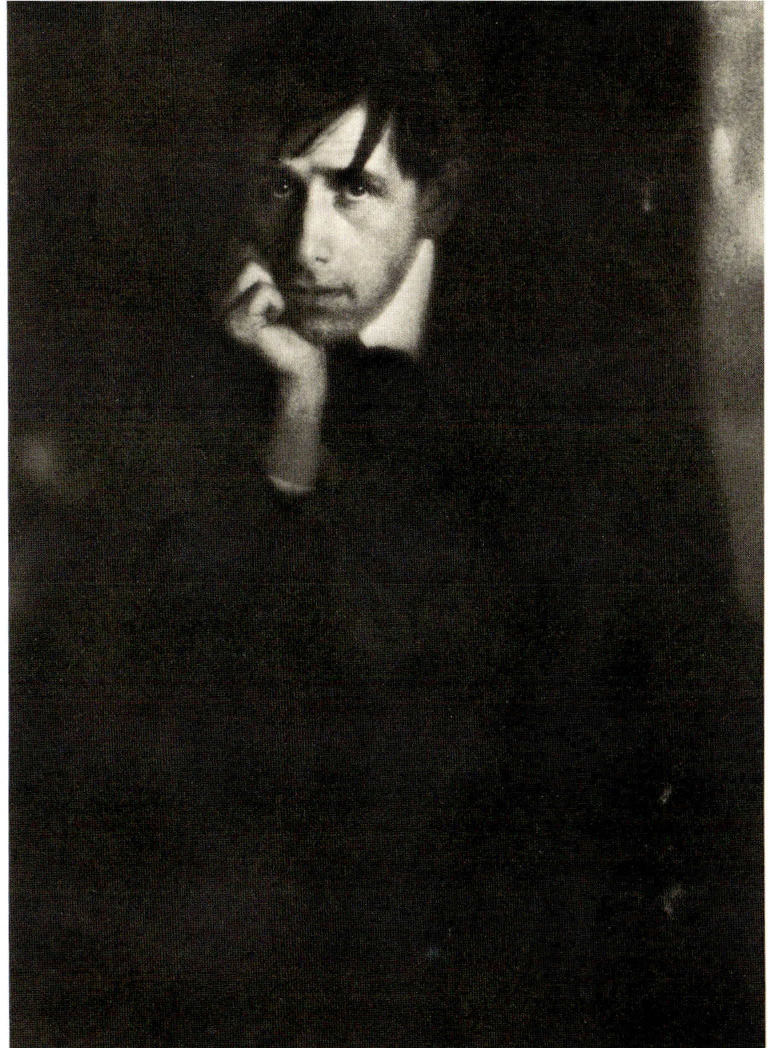

19. Alfred Horsley Hinton,
Beyond, 1905

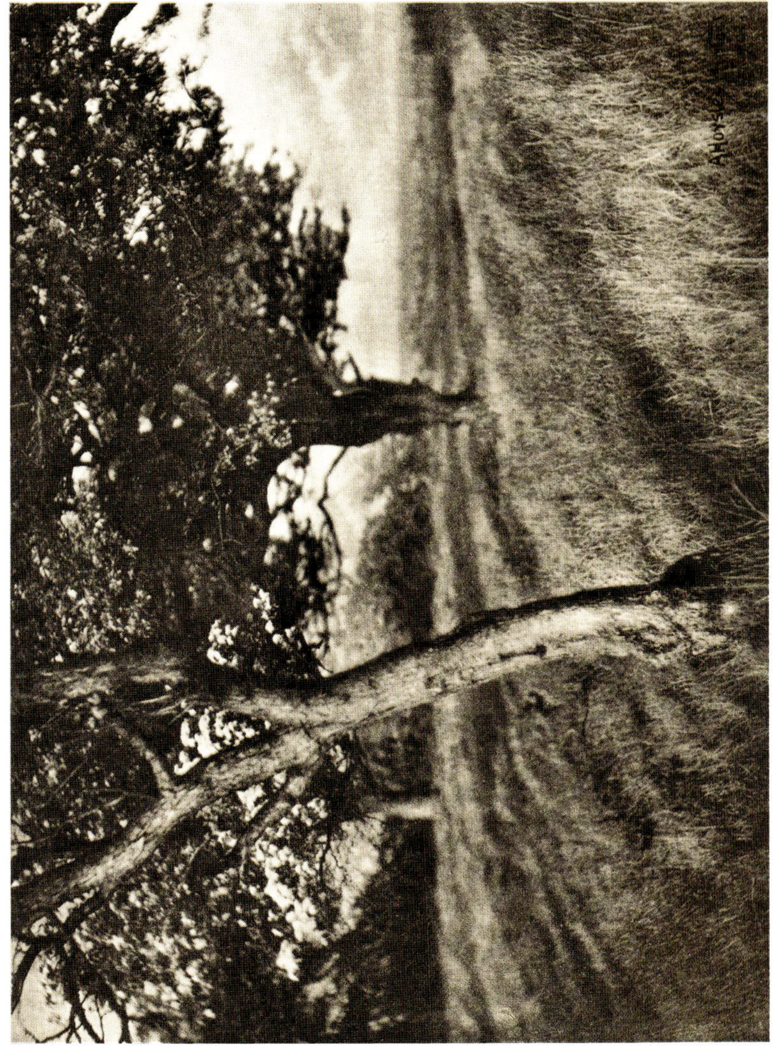

20. Clarence H. White,
The Orchard, 1905

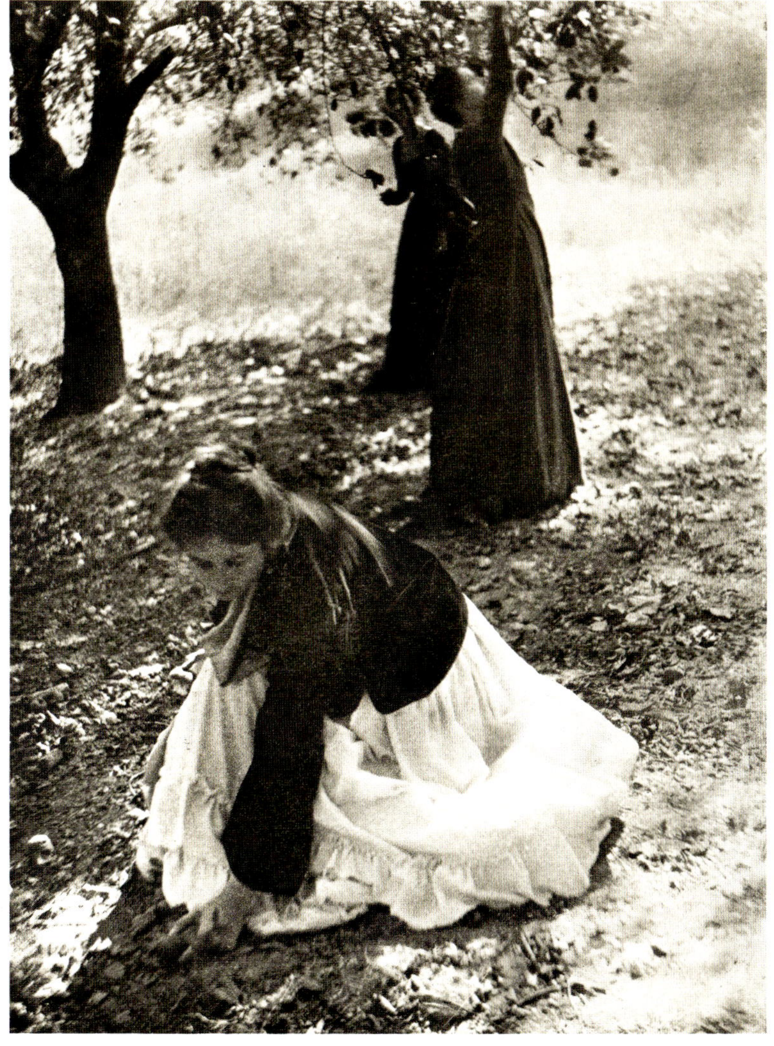

21. Arthur E. Becher,
Moonlight, 1903

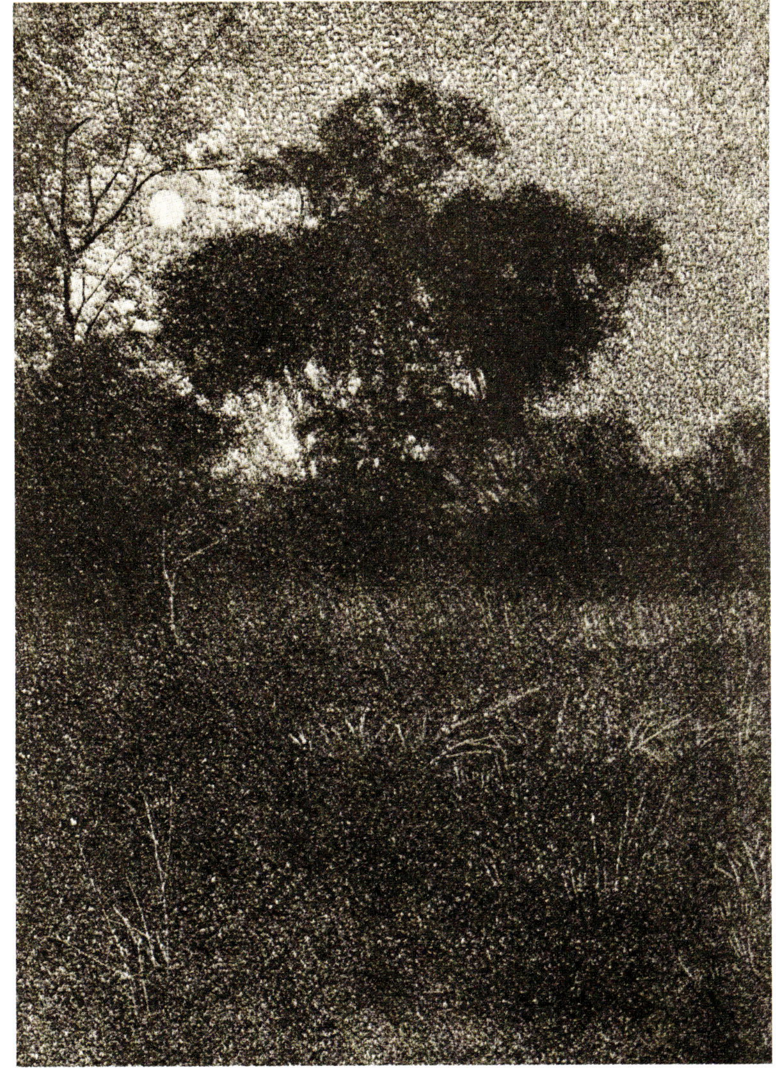

22. Theodor and Oscar Hofmeister,
The Solitary Horseman, 1904

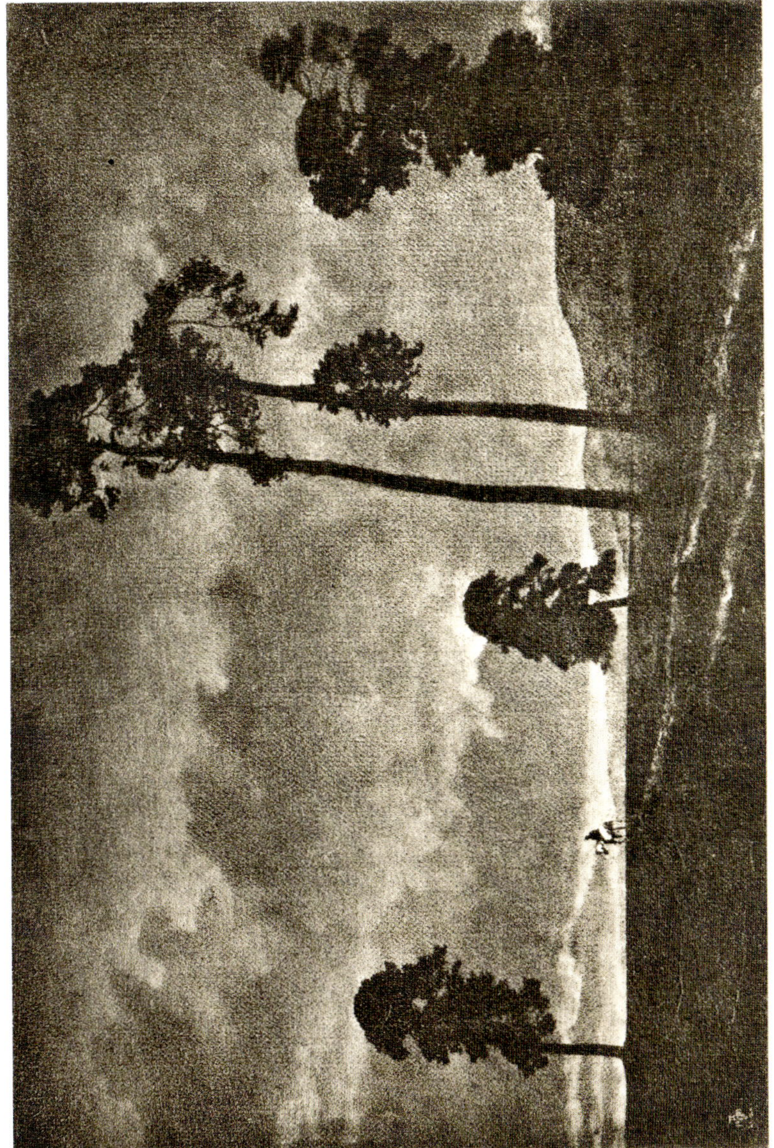

23. Frank Eugene,
Adam and Eve, 1910

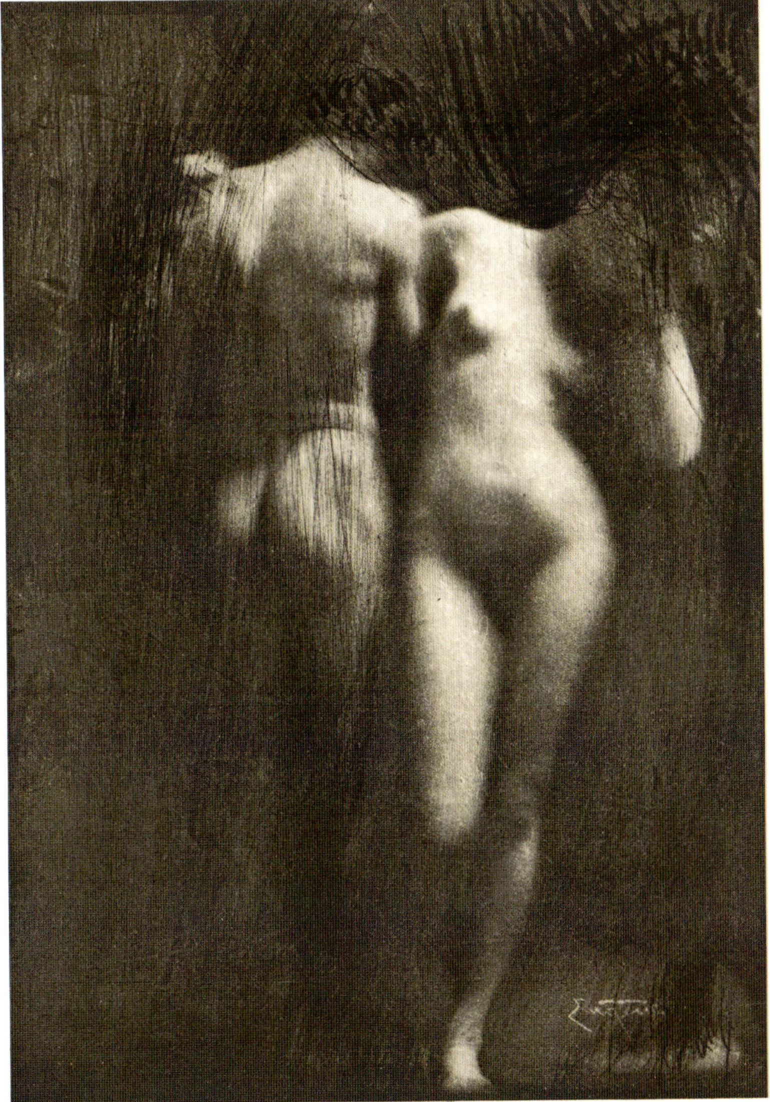

24. Robert Demachy,
Toucques Valley, 1906

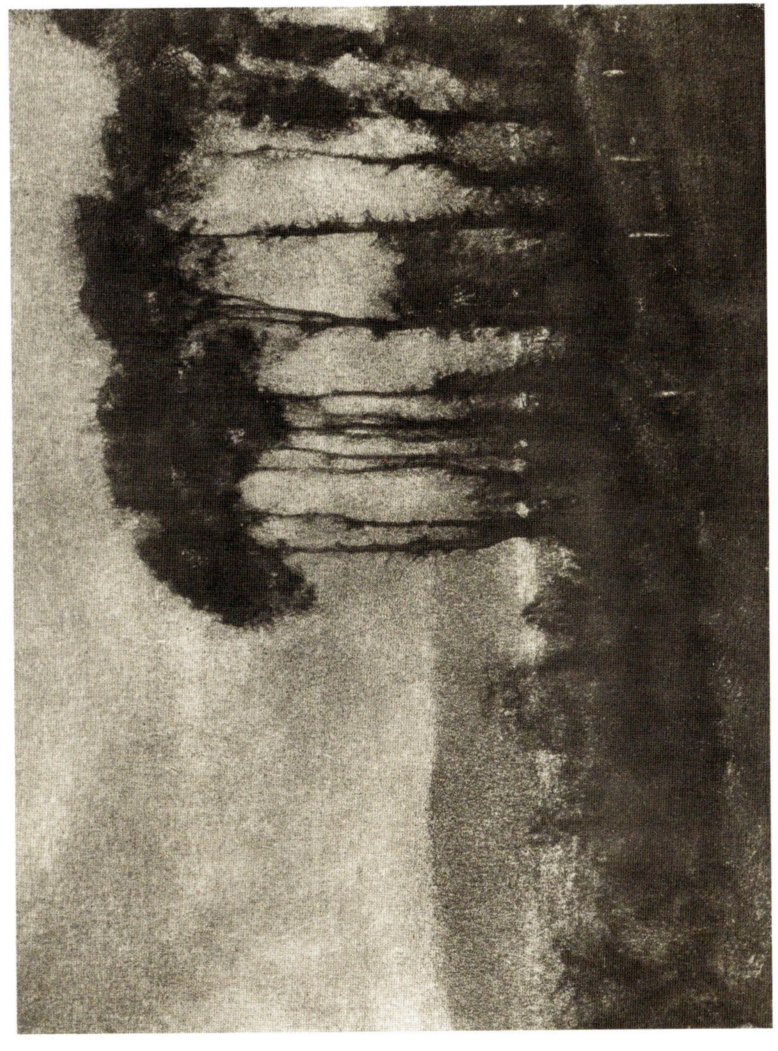

25. Edward J. Steichen,
In Memoriam, 1906

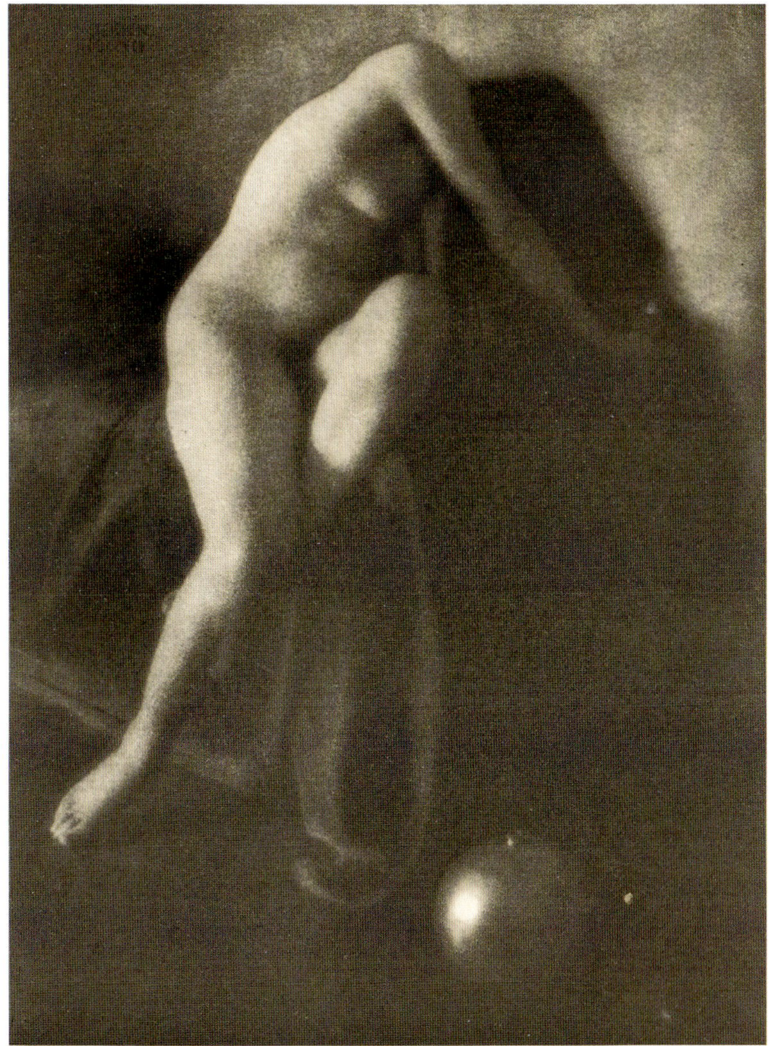

26. David Octavius Hill (and Robert Adamson),
John Gibson Lockhart, 1905

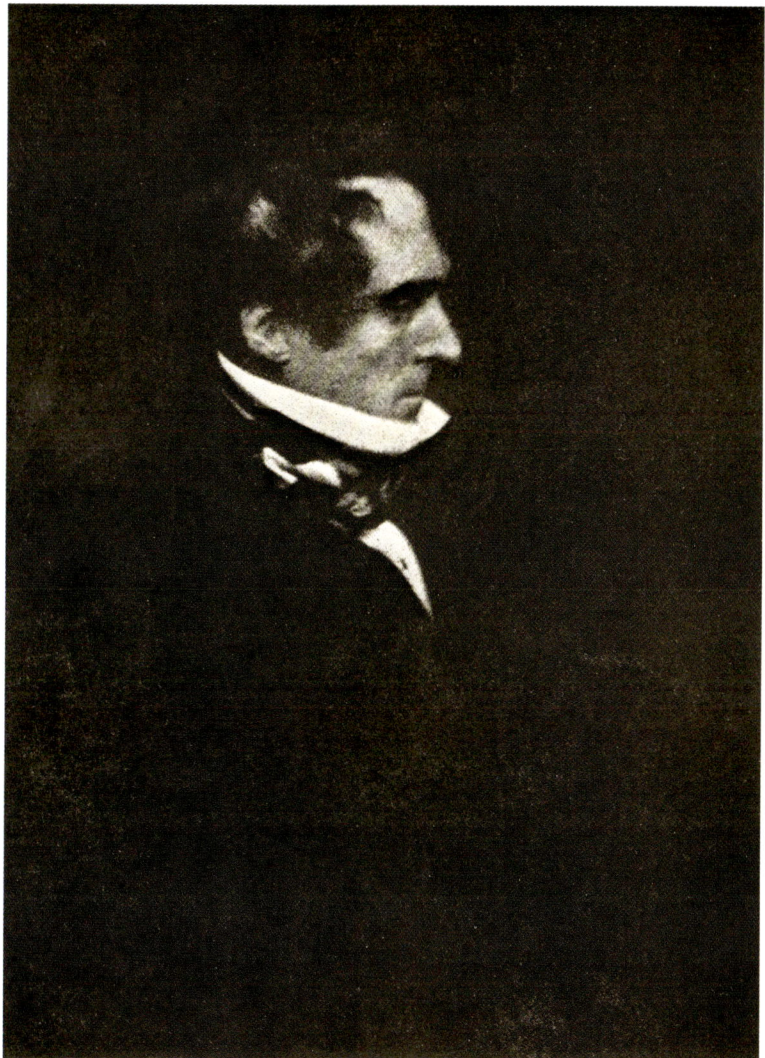

27. Frederick H. Evans,
Ely Cathedral: A Memory of the Normans, 1903

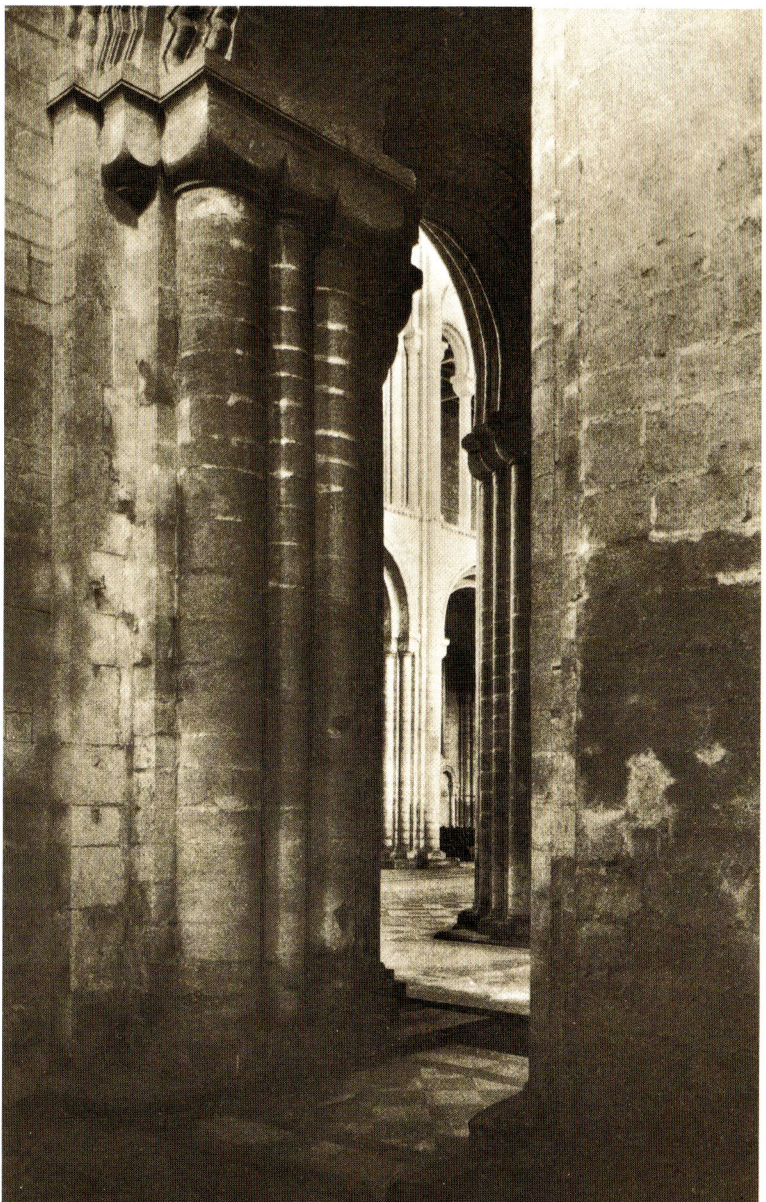

28. David Octavius Hill (and Robert Adamson),
The Bird-Cage, 1909

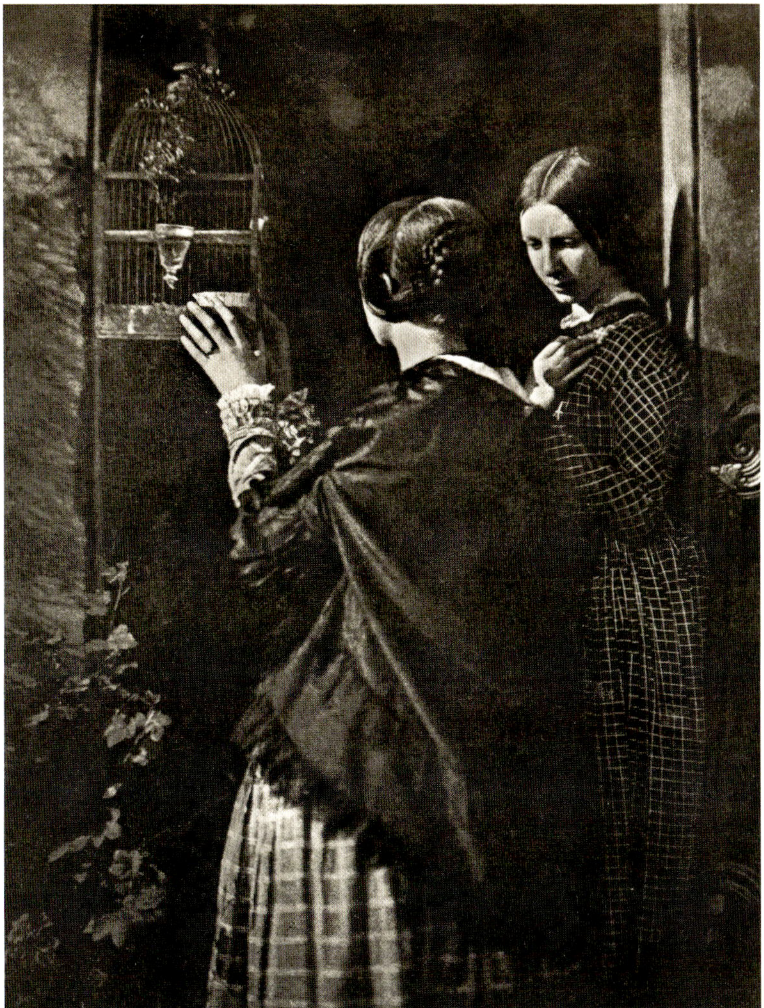

29. Alvin Langdon Coburn,
Spider-webs, 1908

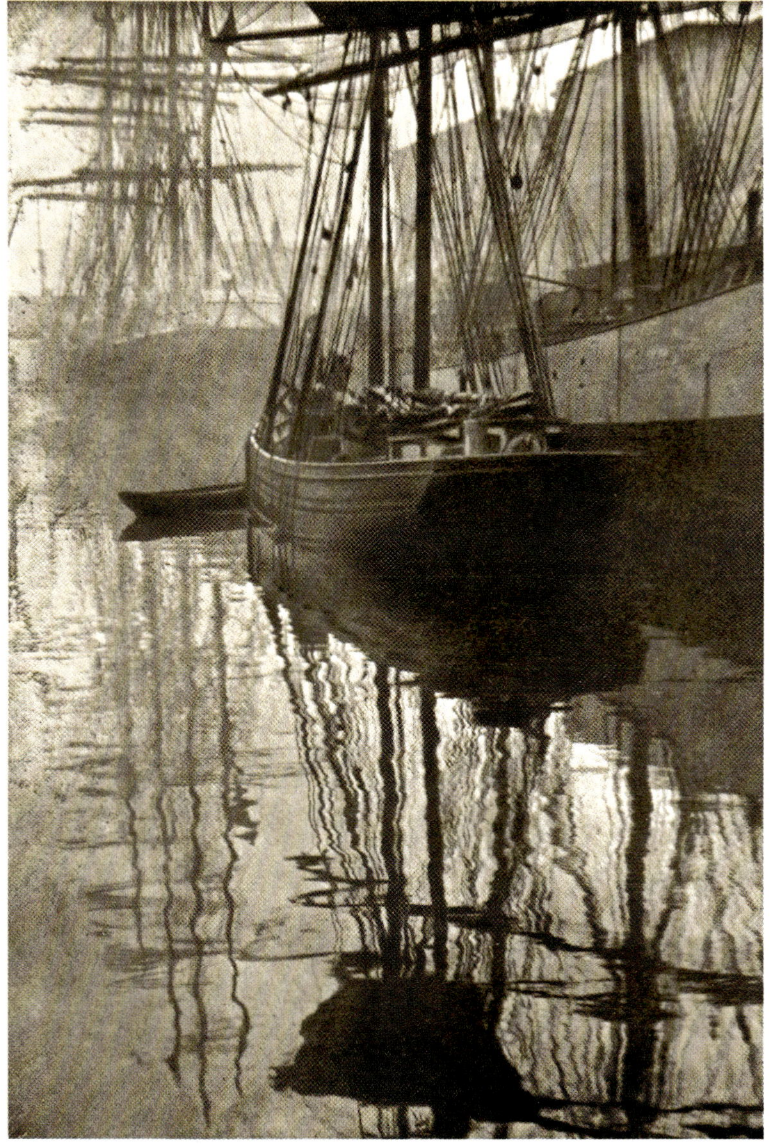

30. Heinrich Kuehn,
On the Shore, 1911

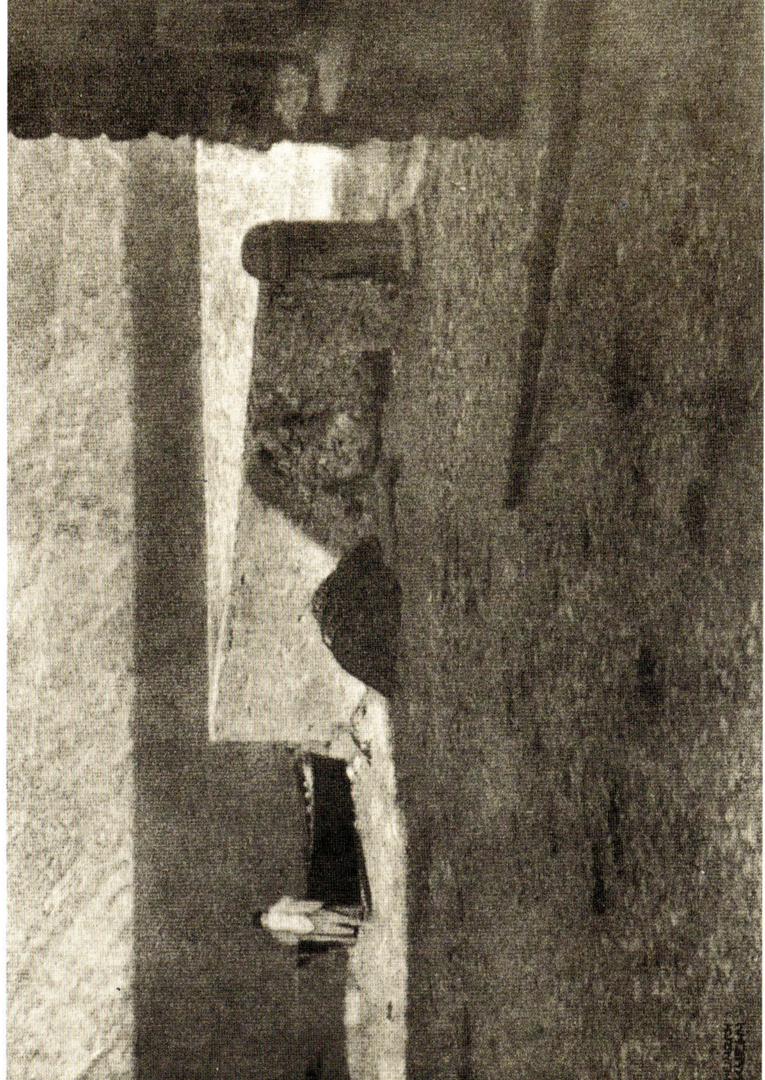

31. Robert Demachy,
Street in Mentone, 1904

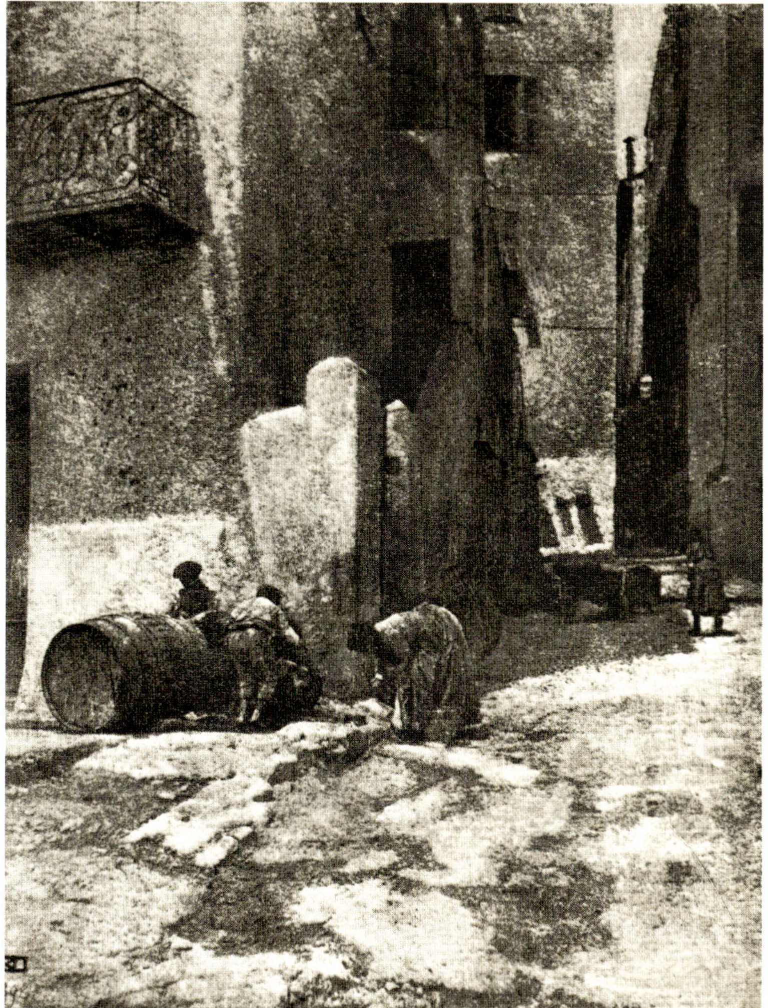

32. J. Craig Annan,
Stirling Castle, 1907

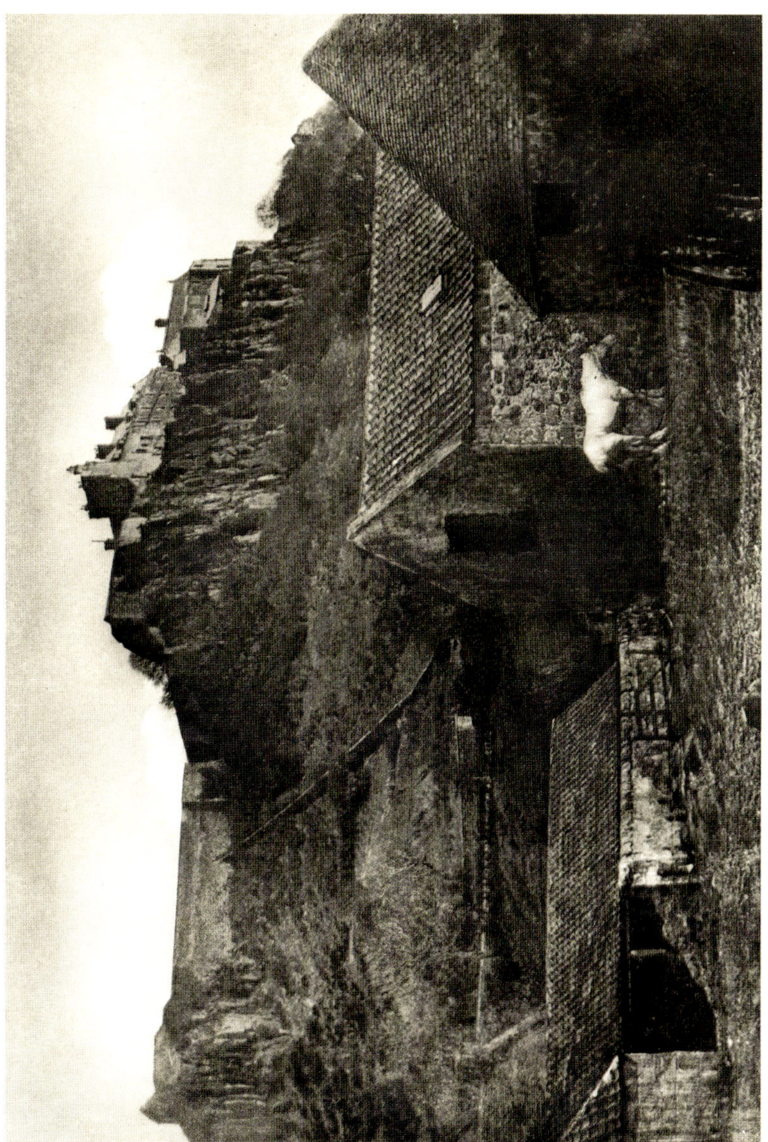

33. Adolf de Meyer,
Mrs. Wiggins of Belgrave Square, 1912

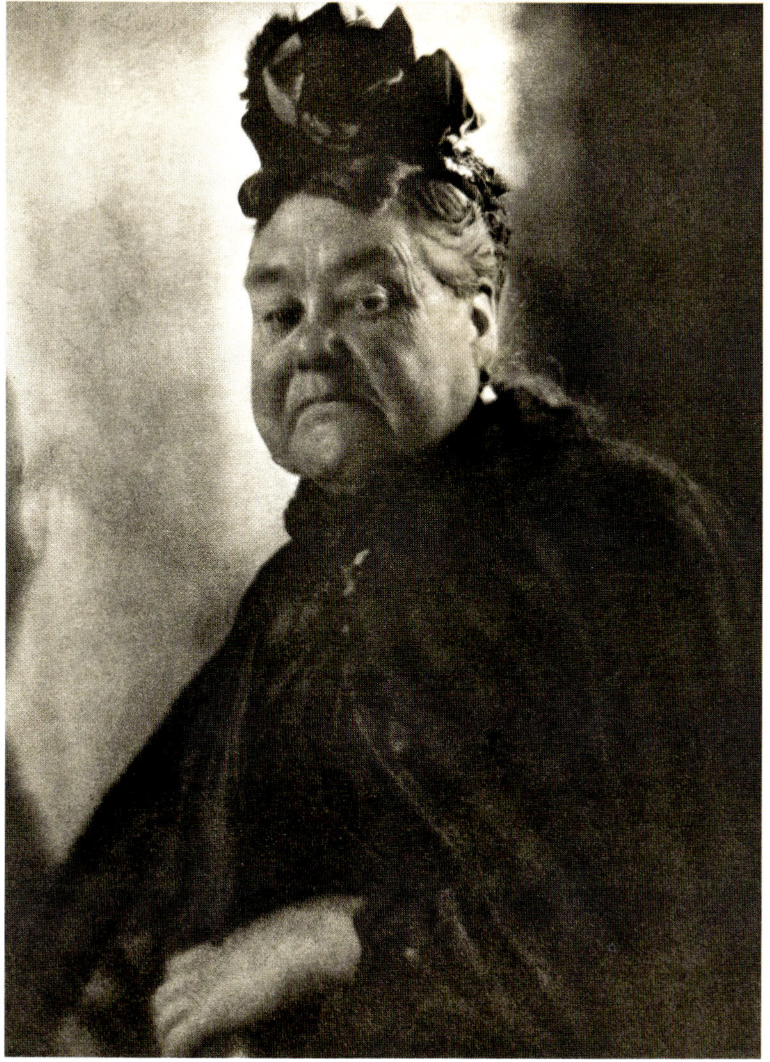

34. Alvin Langdon Coburn,
Wier's Close – Edinburgh, 1906

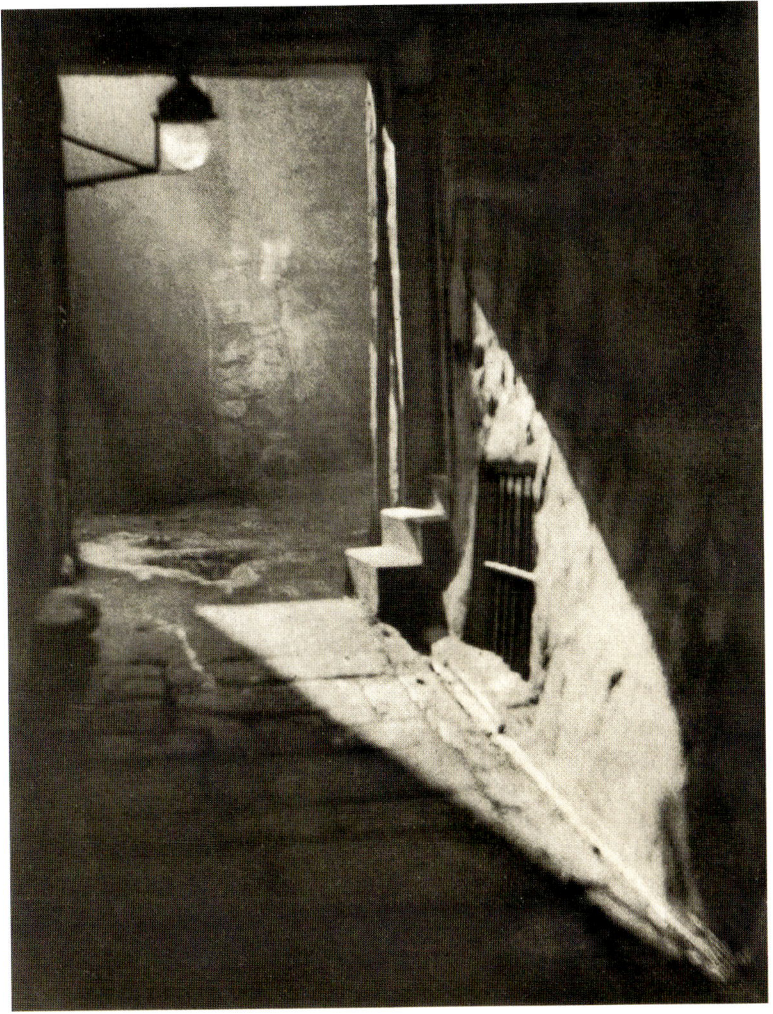

35. Edward J. Steichen,
Balzac – The Open Sky, 1911

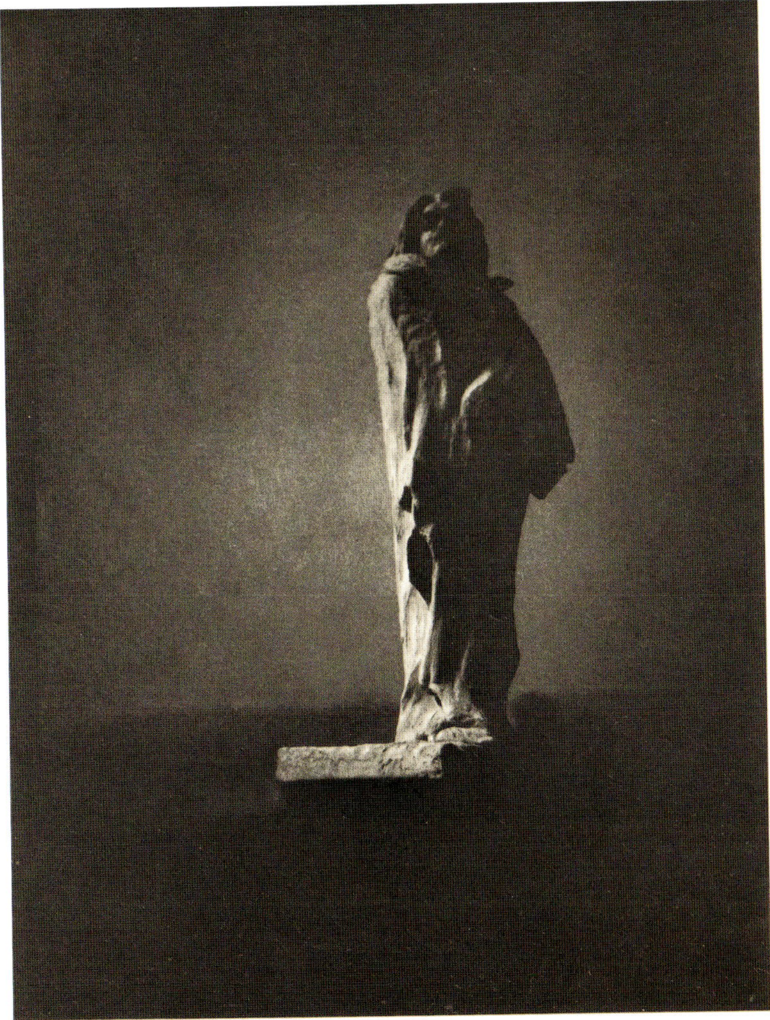

36. Julia Margaret Cameron,
Herschel, 1913

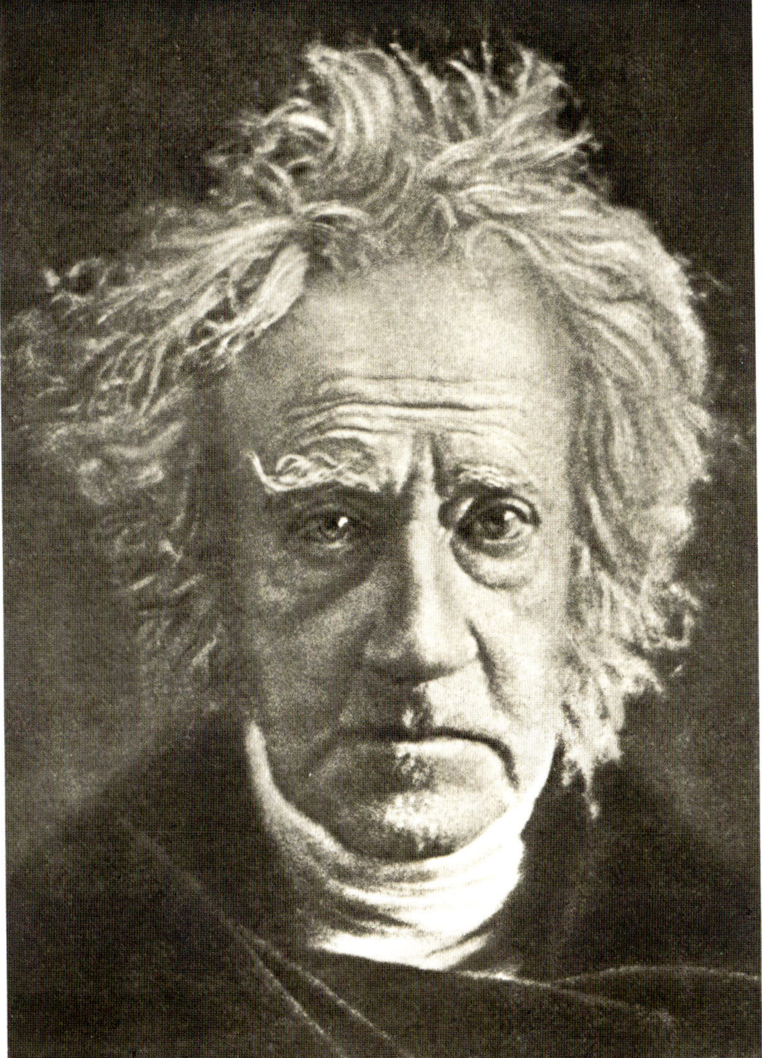

37. Edward J. Steichen,
Rodin, 1903

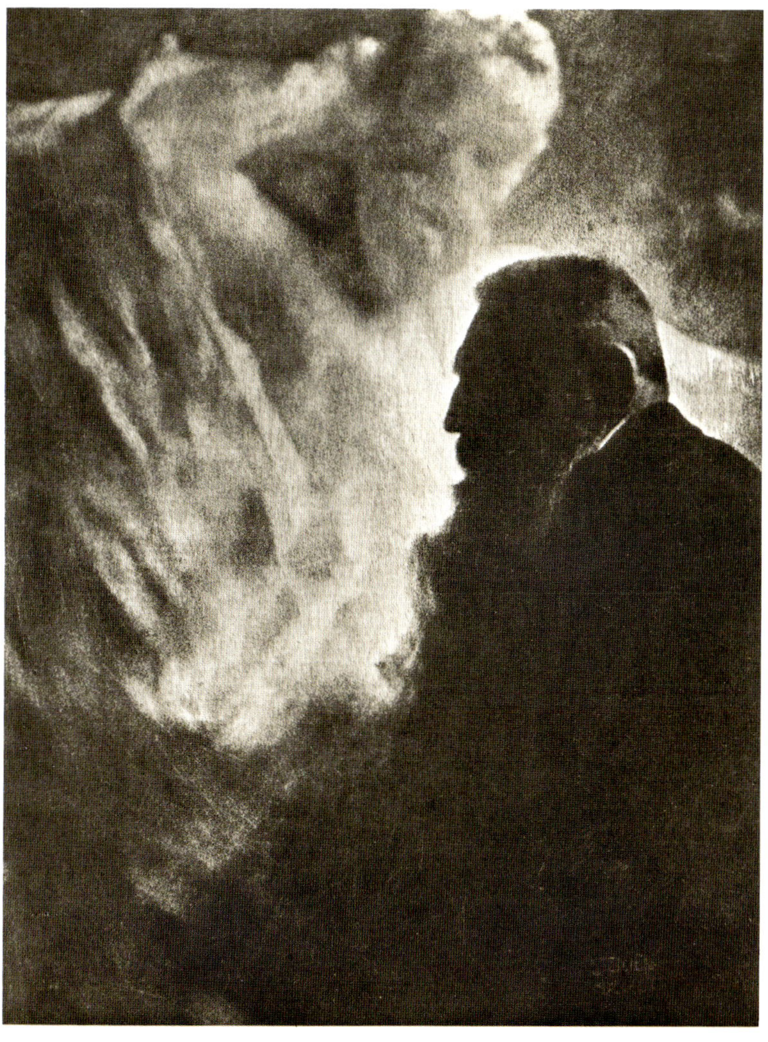

38. Alvin Langdon Coburn,
The Bridge, Venice, 1908

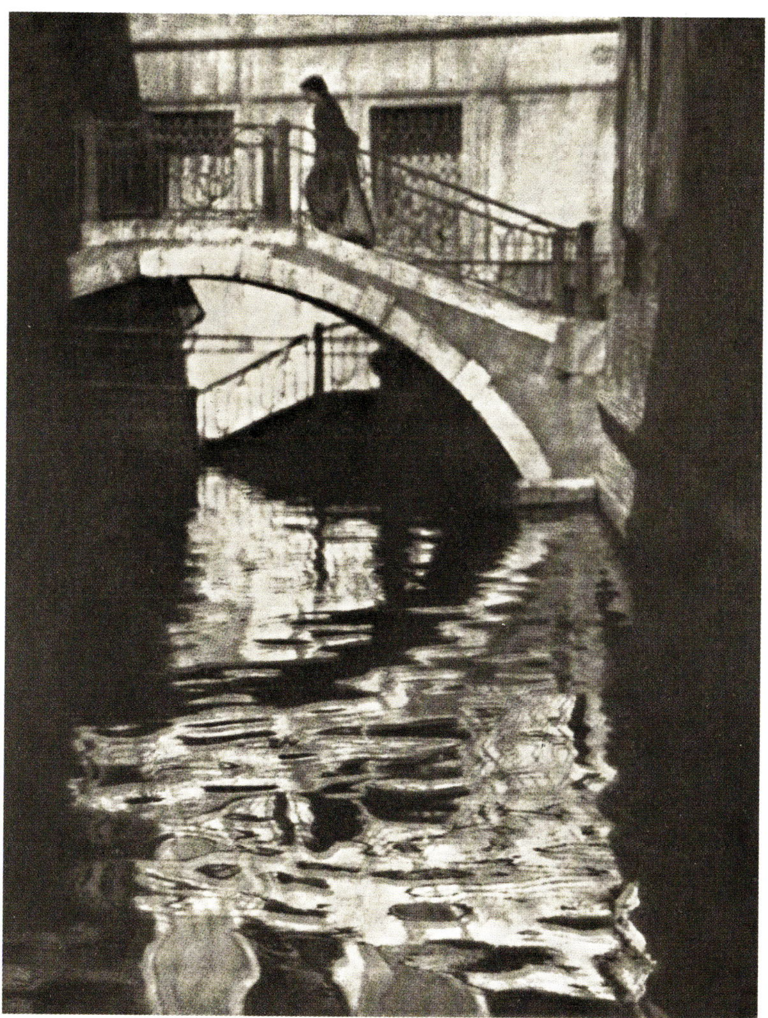

39. Edward J. Steichen,
Cyclamen – Mrs. Philip Lydig, 1913

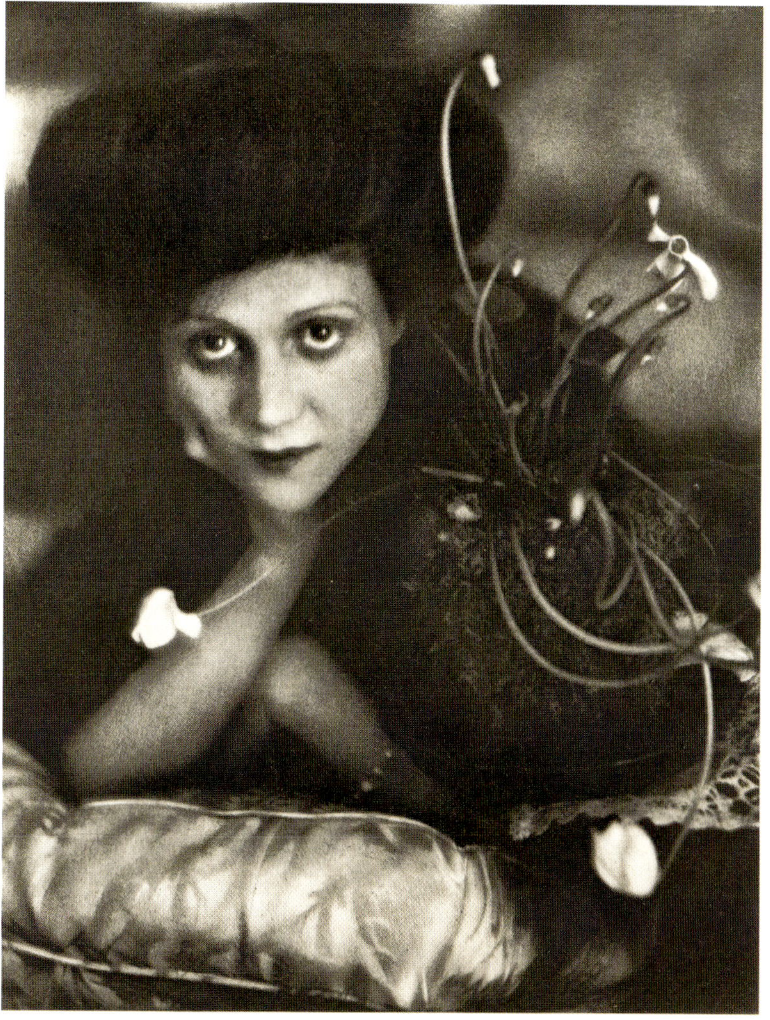

40. Clarence H. White,
Drops of Rain, 1908

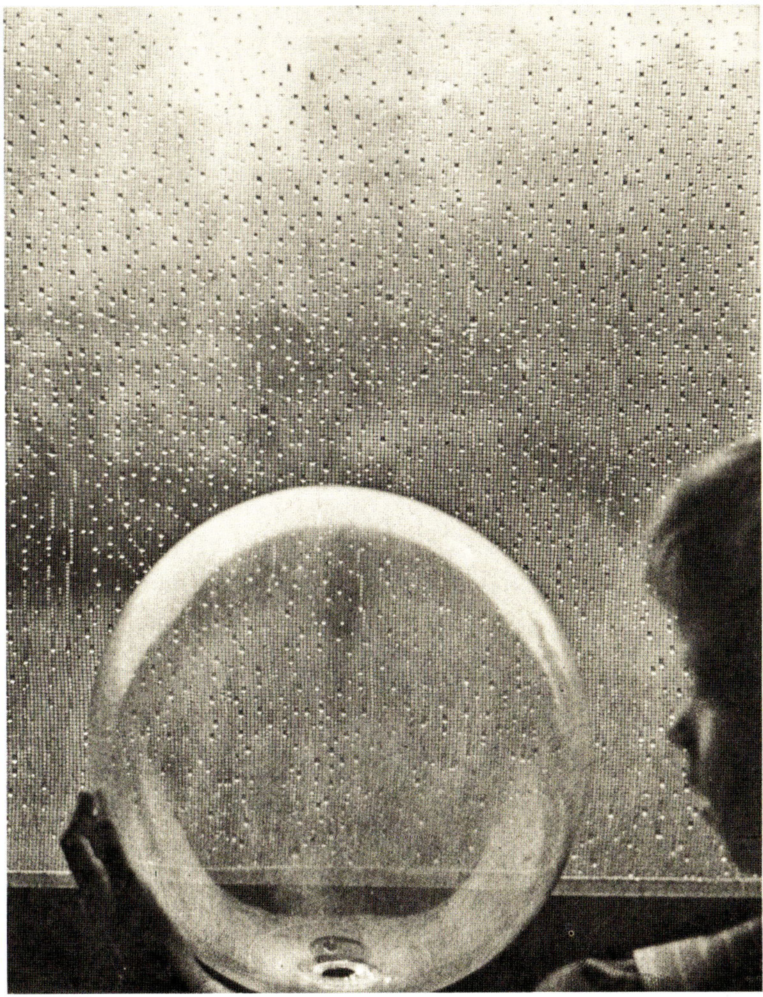

41. George H. Seeley,
Blotches of Sunlight and Spots of Ink, 1907

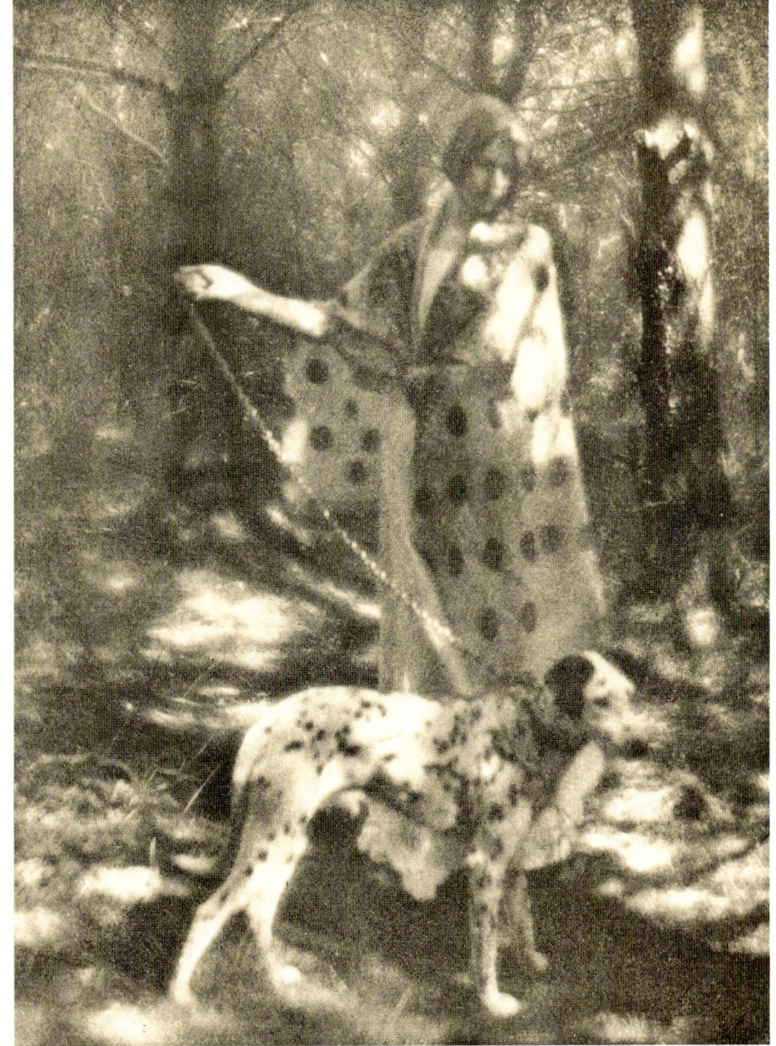

42. Frank Eugene,
Frau Ludwig von Hohlwein, 1910

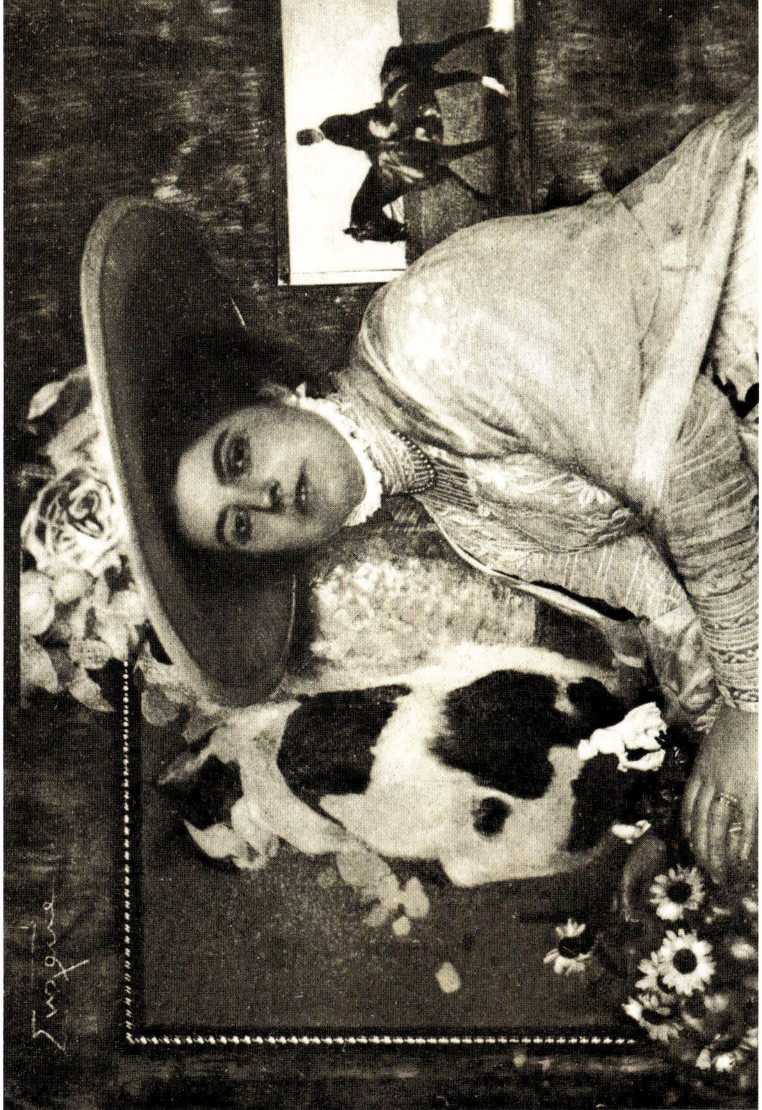

43. Adolf de Meyer,
Glass and Shadows, 1912

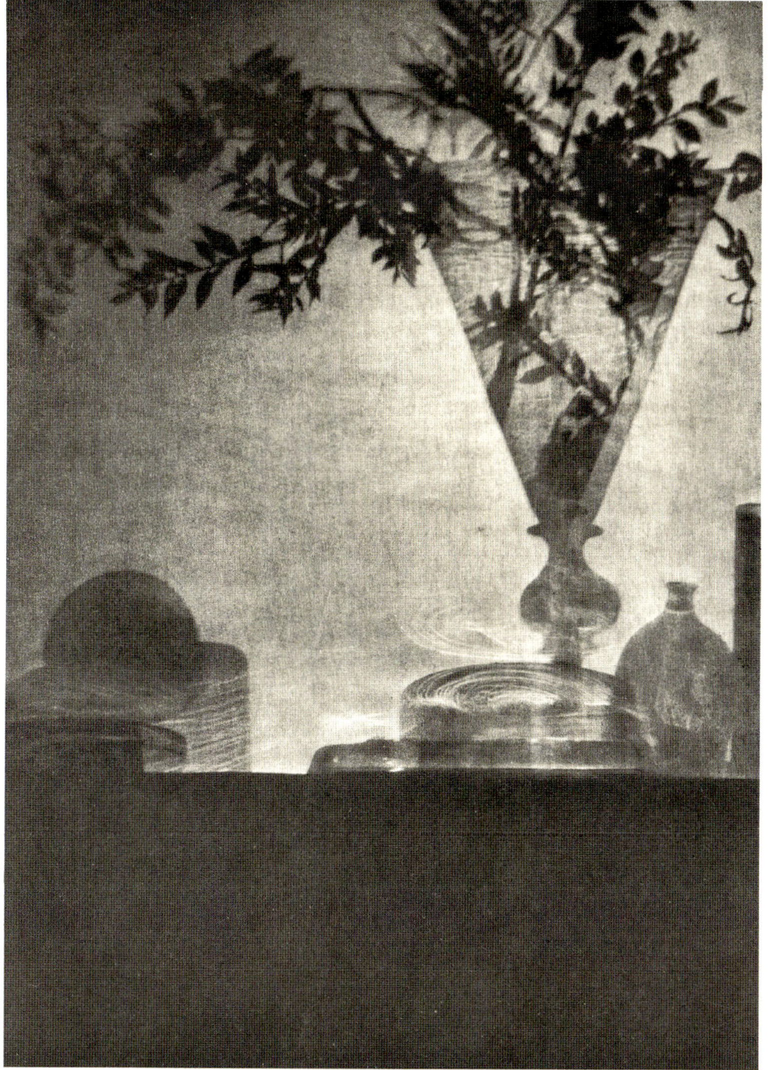

44. Adolf de Meyer,
The Cup, 1912

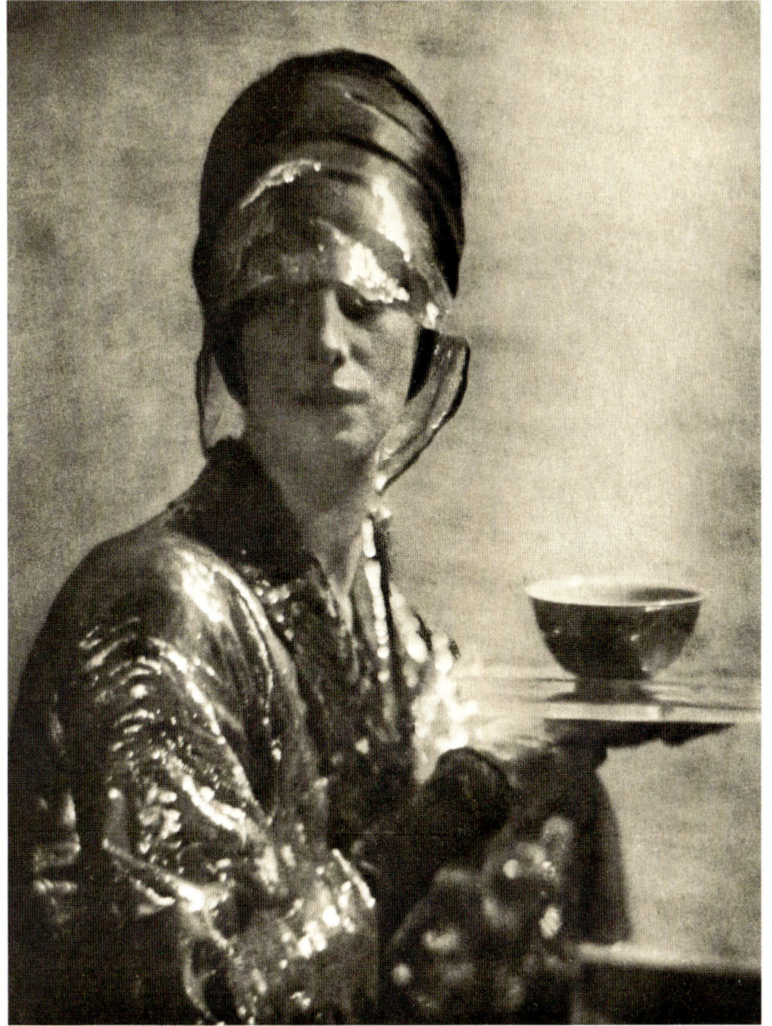

45. Edward J. Steichen,
Steeplechase Day, Paris; Grand Stand, 1913

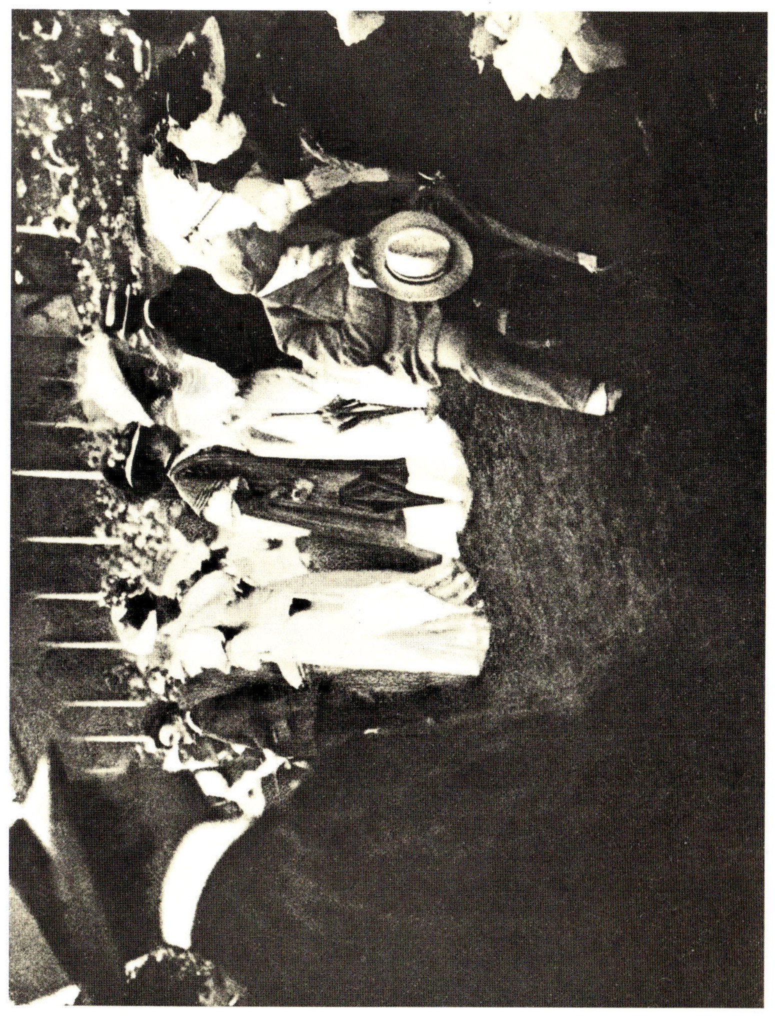

46. Alfred Stieglitz,
Going to the Start (1904), 1905

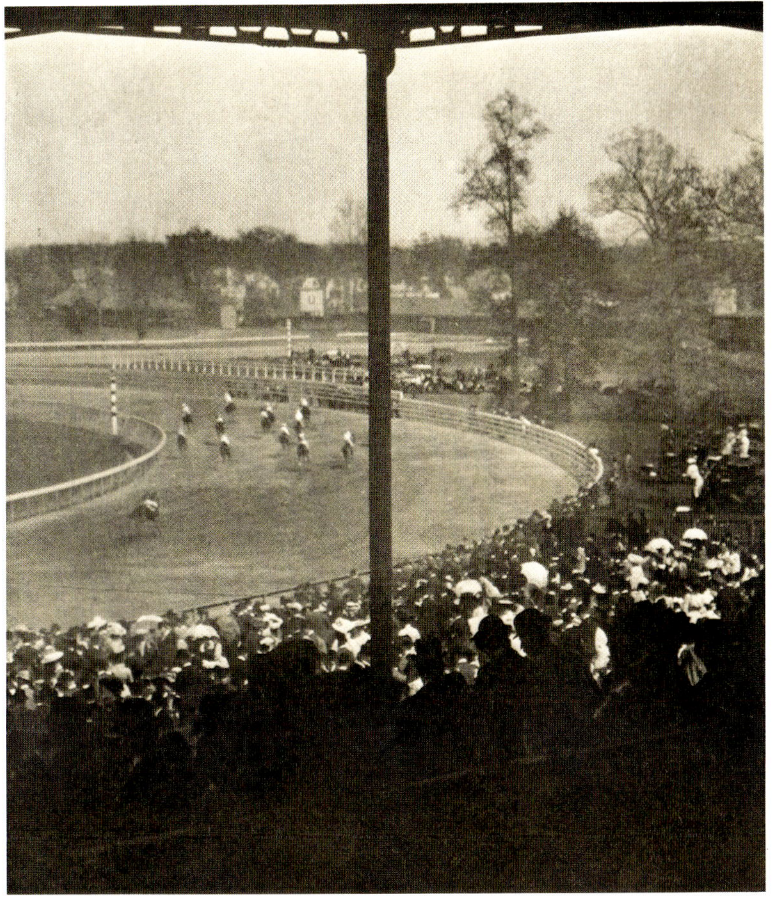

47. Edward J. Steichen,
Steeplechase Day, Paris; After the Races, 1913

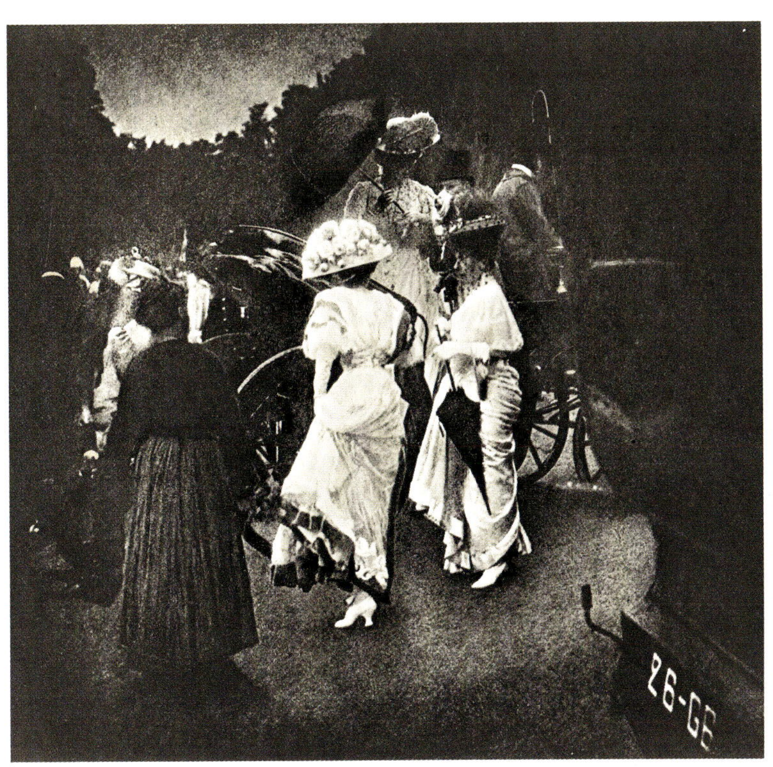

48. Harry C. Rubincam,
In the Circus, 1907

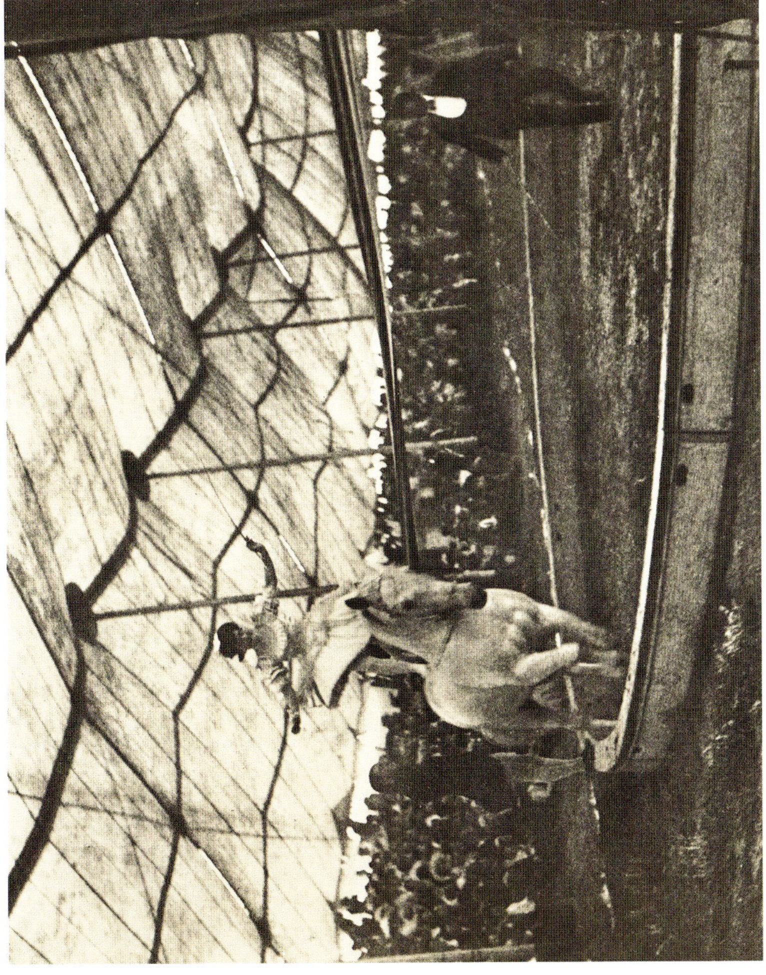

49. Gertrude Käsebier,
Portrait (Miss N.), 1903

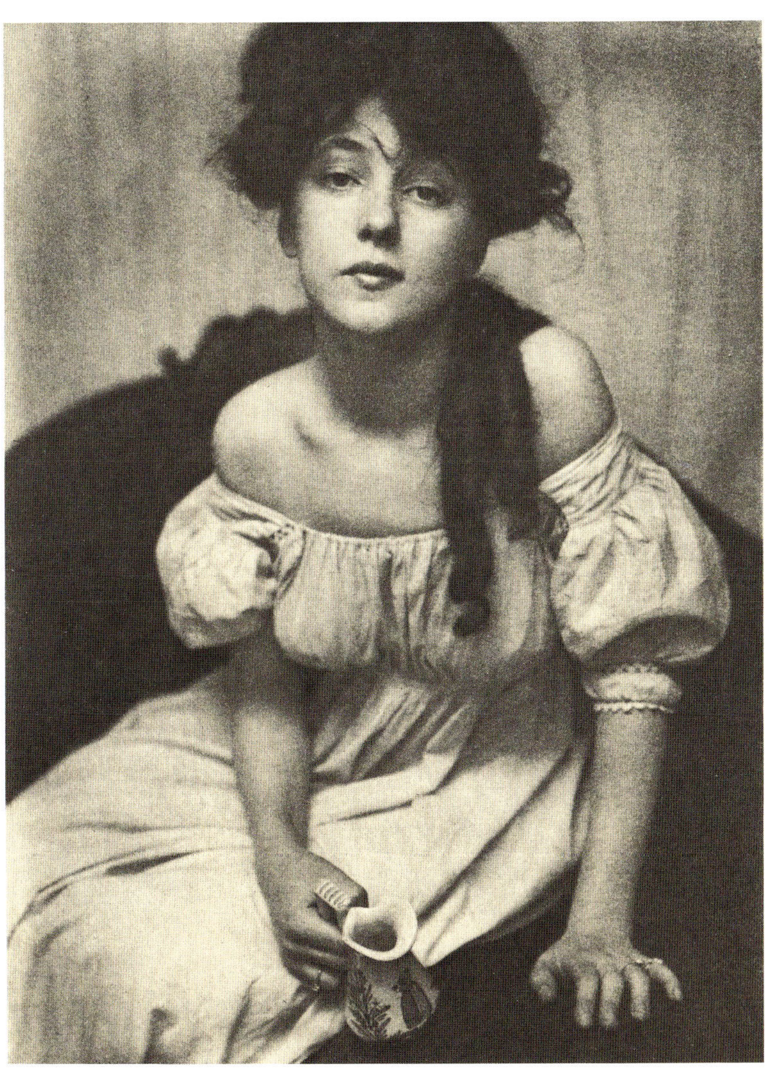

50. Alfred Stieglitz,
A Snapshot; Paris (1911), 1913

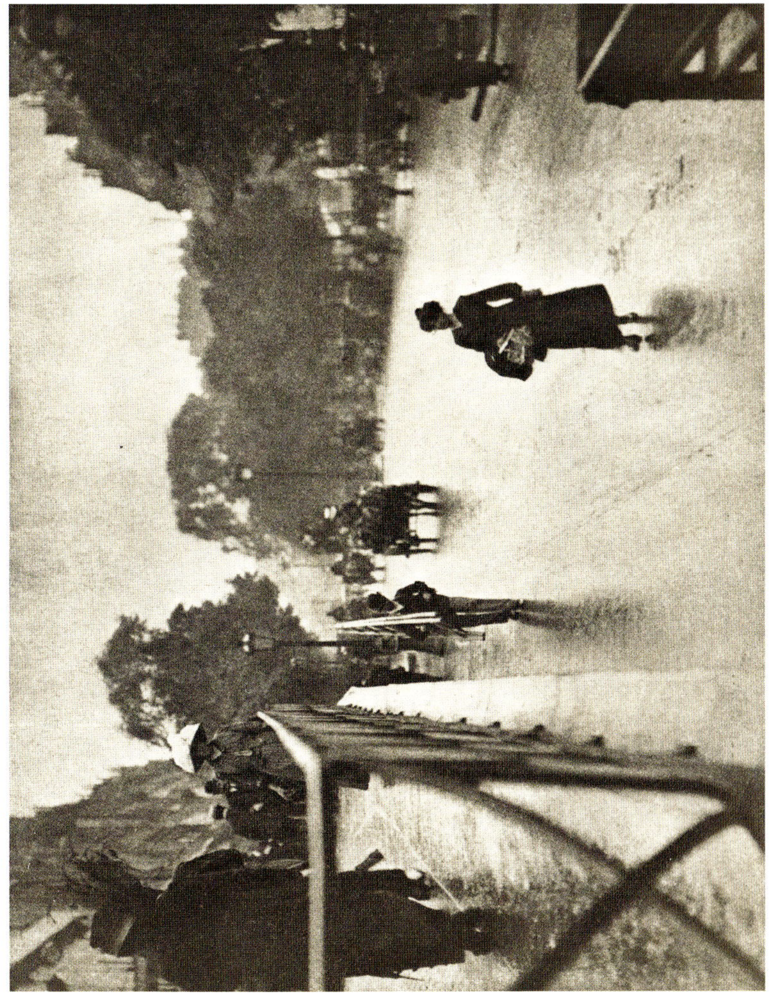

51. Alfred Stieglitz,
Spring Showers, New York (1900), 1911

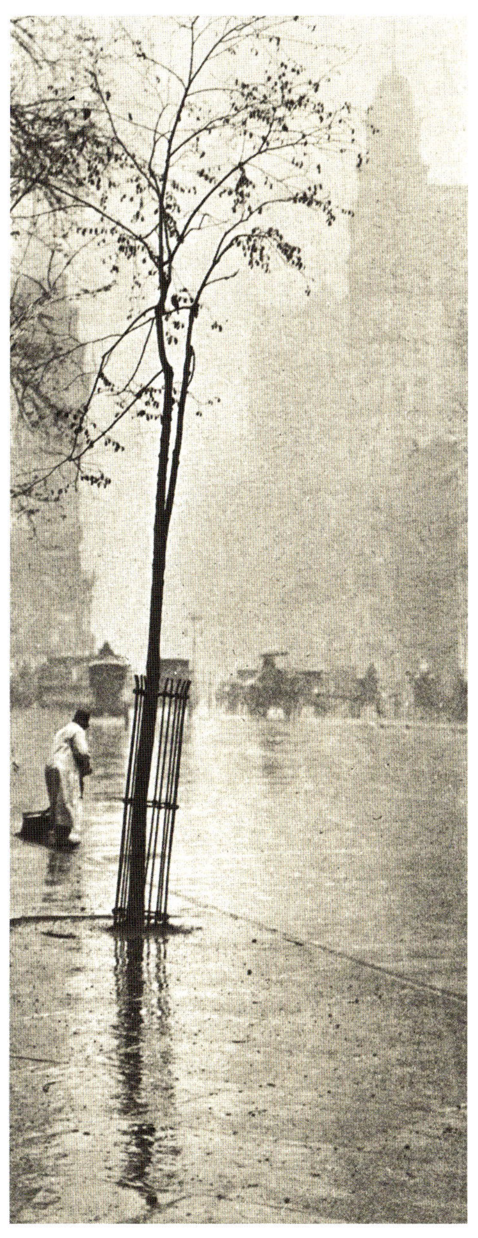

52. Constant Puyo,
Montmartre, 1906

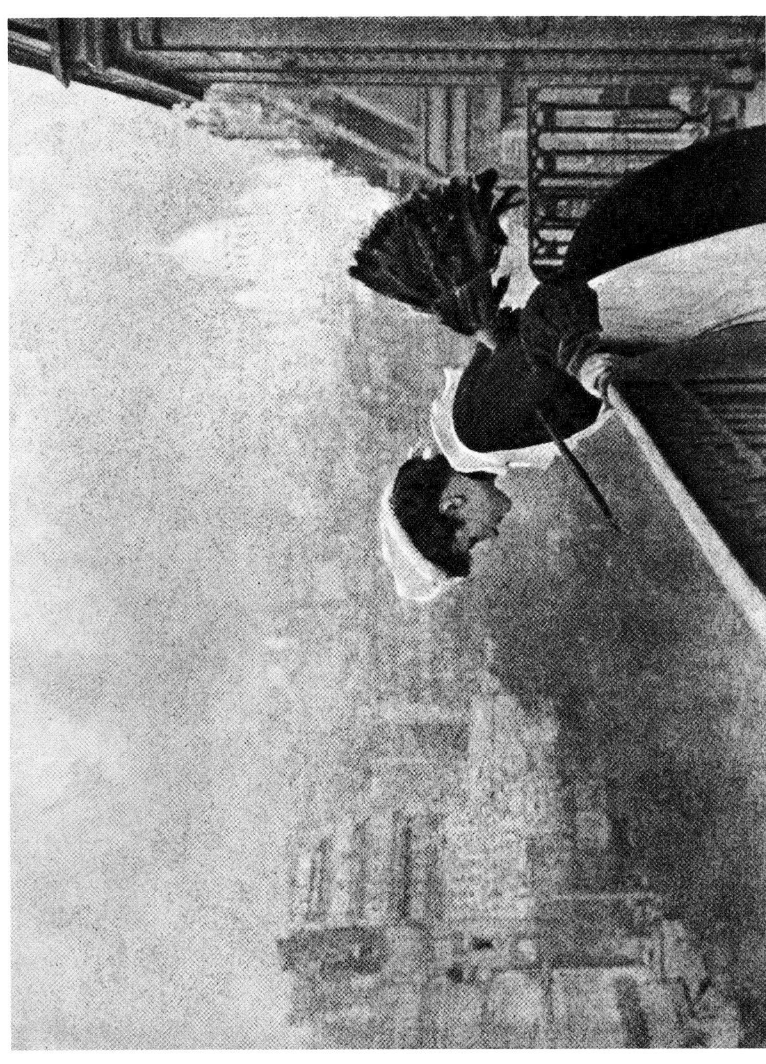

53. Alfred Stieglitz,
Detail: Picasso-Braque Exhibition (January, 1915), 1916

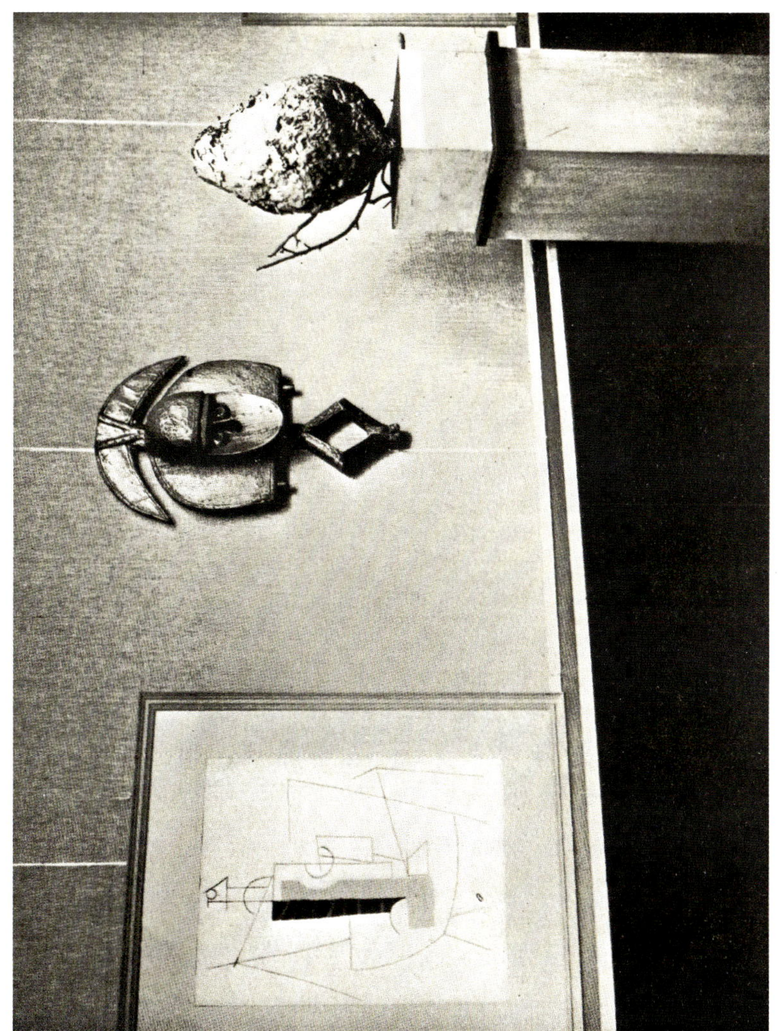

54. Edward J. Steichen,
The Flatiron – Evening, 1906

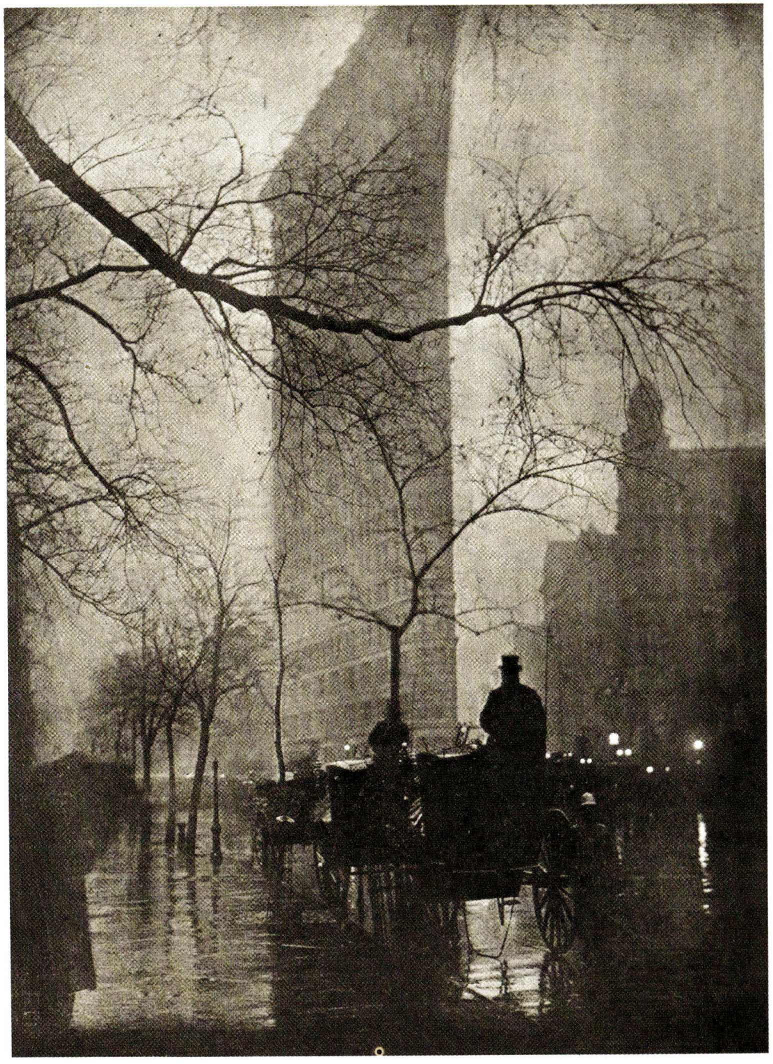

55. Alfred Stieglitz,
Brancusi Sculpture (March, 1914), 1916

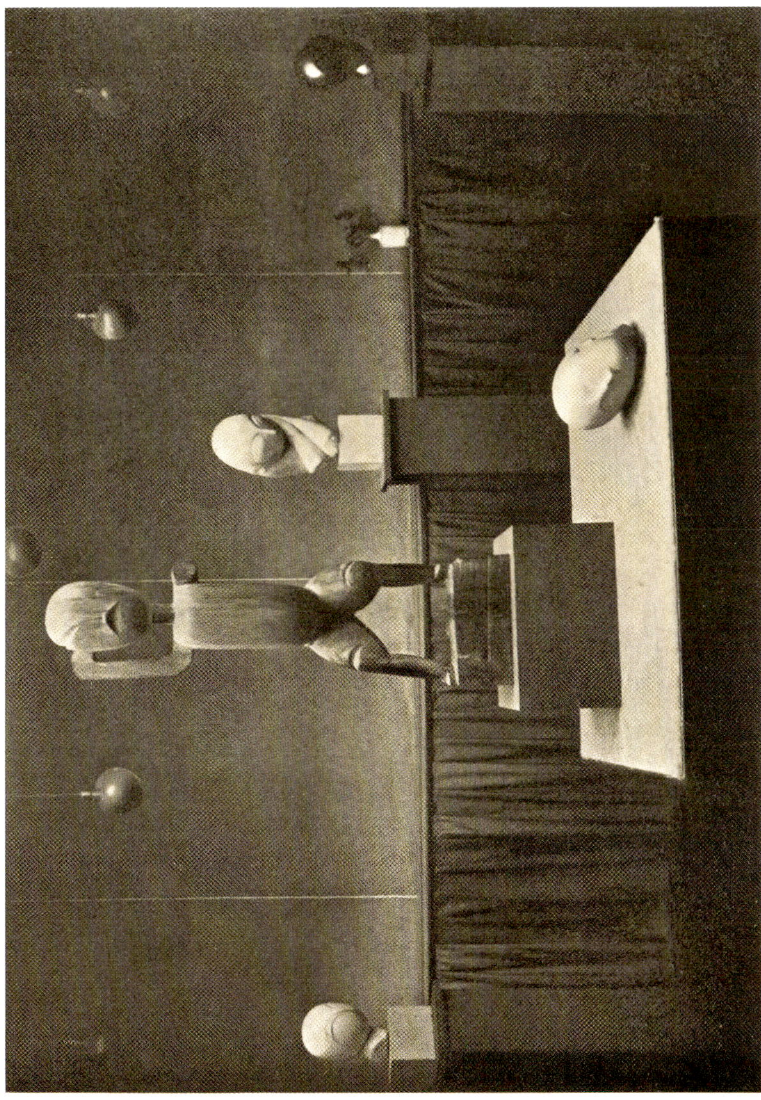

56. Alfred Stieglitz,
The Steerage (1907), 1911

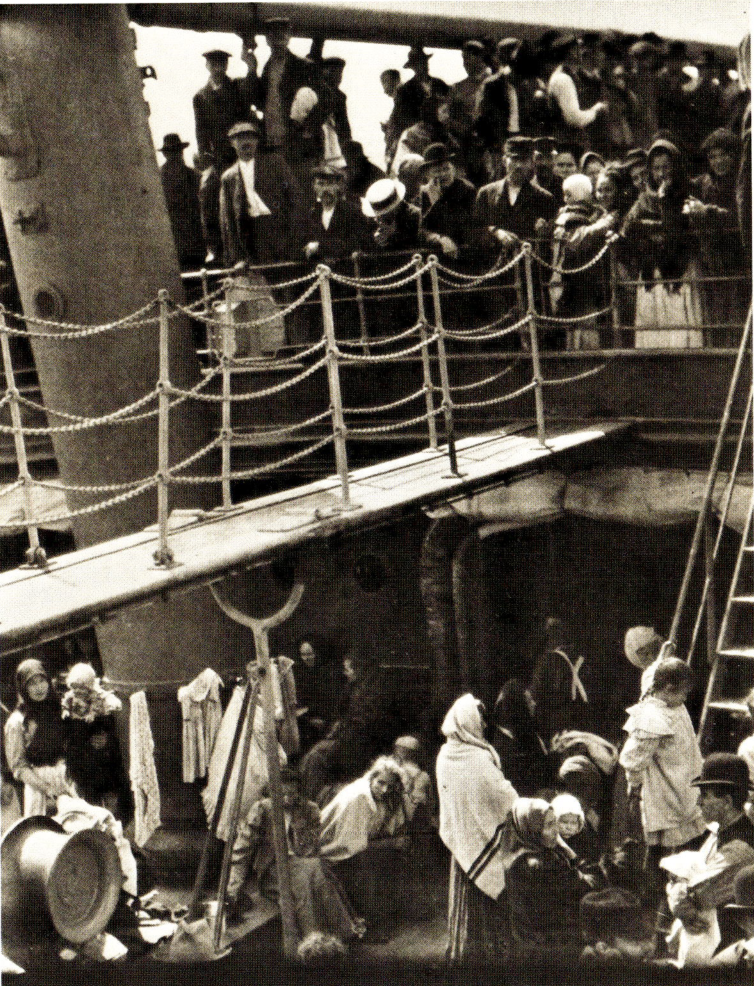

57. Paul B. Haviland,
Passing Steamer, 1912

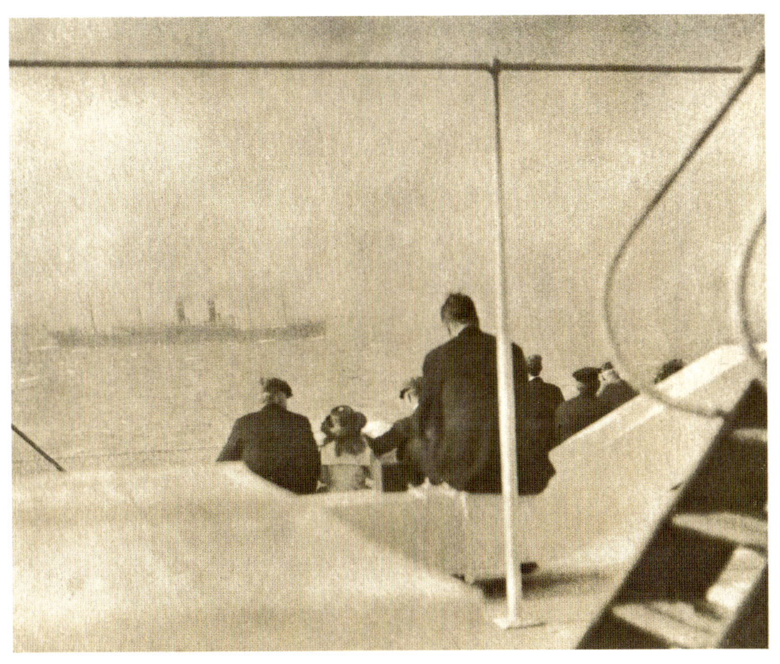

58. Alfred Stieglitz,
Snapshot – From my Window, New York, 1907

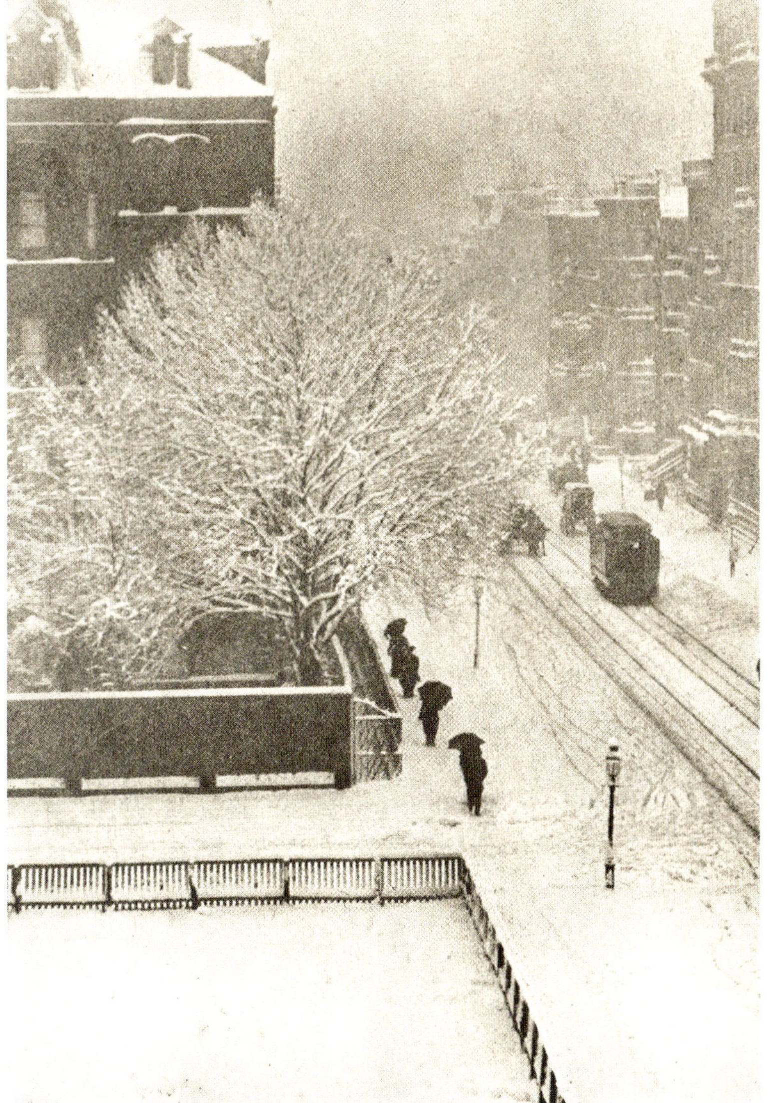

59. Paul Strand,
Photograph, 1917

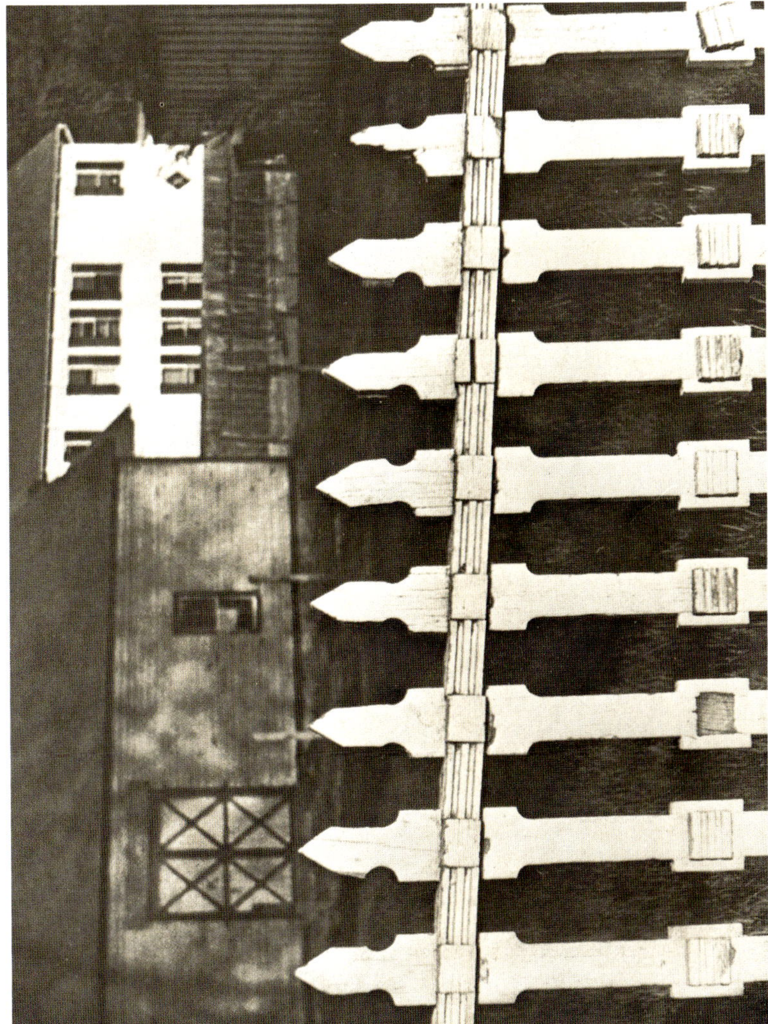

60. Paul Strand,
Photograph – New York, 1917

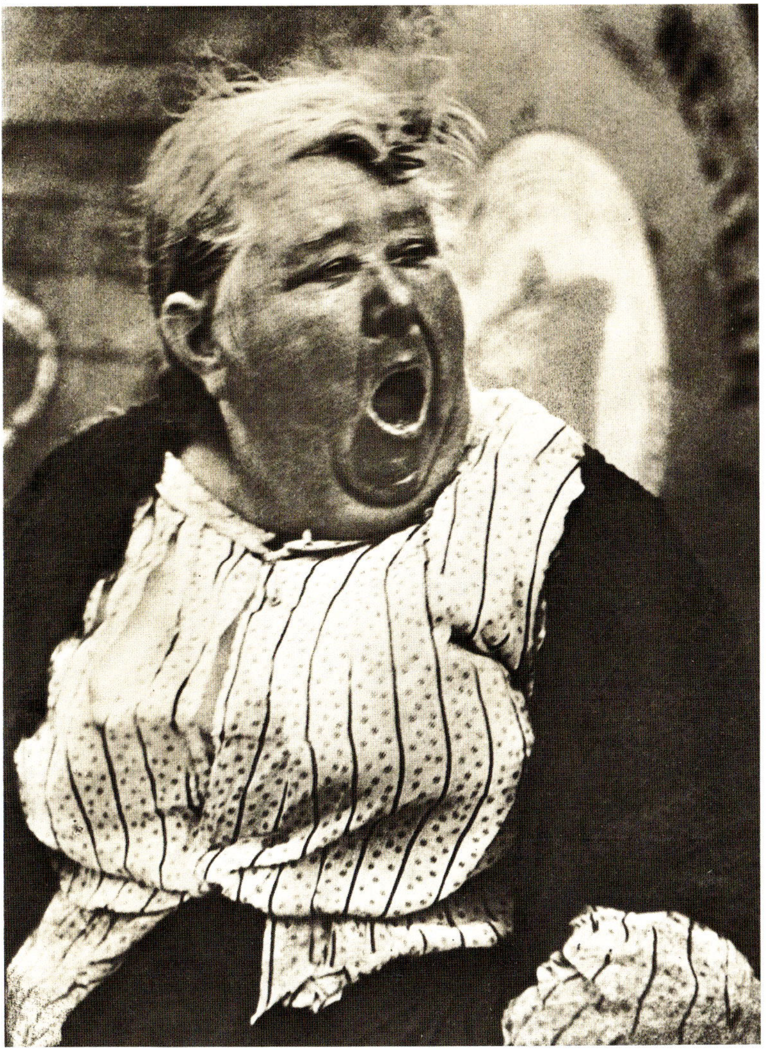

61. Paul Strand,
Photograph, 1917

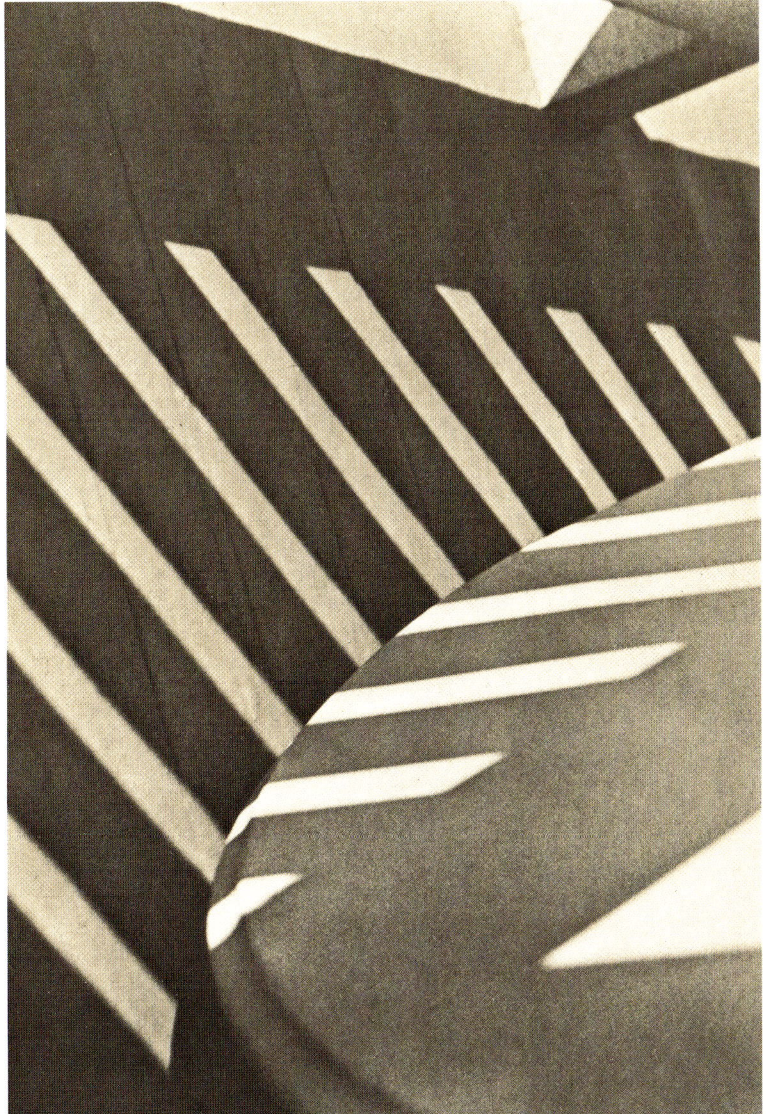

THE MAGAZINE *CAMERA WORK*

Fifty issues of *Camera Work* appeared between 1903 and 1917. With a few exceptions, the magazine was published in quarterly numbers until 1913; however, only three numbers appeared in 1914, none at all in 1915, and only one in 1916, while the last appearance was in the form of a double issue (numbers 49/50) in 1917. Some other numbers were also published as double issues (for instance, numbers 34/35 in 1911 and 42/43 in 1913). In addition, there were special supplementary numbers from time to time (for instance, one on Steichen in 1906 and one on Matisse in 1912). The magazine was in quarto format (approximately 29 x 21 cm) and had a print run of 1,000. The price of the annual subscription was originally $4 (and $2 for a single number) in 1903, immediately rising to $5 (and $3) in 1904, and eventually to $8 in 1913, with the price of single numbers varying from $2 to $8 throughout the years of publication. Each issue comprised fifty pages on average, including advertising, with between ten and fourteen full-page reproductions devoted to the work of one or two artists. The texts entailed critical reviews and, depending on length, between three and seven articles on aesthetics in the field of photography and the other arts. These articles were deliberately unconnected with the illustrative material and tended to be polemical in content.

The reproductions, which were of a remarkably high quality, were mostly printed by the firm of Bruckmann in Munich or by the Manhattan Photogravure Company in New York, and sometimes by other firms such as Waddington (London) and Annan (Glasgow). More often than not, they were printed under the supervision of the photographers themselves, some of whom (Steichen among them) retouched the prints by hand. They covered the entire spectrum of photogravure and half-tone reproduction processes in use at the time (see the notes on techniques overleaf).

The decorative layout of *Camera Work* was extremely simple, so that, unlike the Photo-Club de Paris magazine, it strikes a very modern note today. It was quite clearly inspired by Viennese Art Nouveau, while the title lettering (created by Steichen) was based moreover on a Viennese model. Elegant and luxuriously produced, *Camera Work* used materials of the highest quality (rag cover in grey or bronze-green, with deckle edges for the special issues; photogravures generally on Japan tissue). Its sober typography was enlivened by ornamental initials and tailpieces in the Art Nouveau style, and the reproductions were often pasted by hand on double mounts of two shades of grey, brown or cream.

PICTORIALIST PRINTING TECHNIQUES AND REPRODUCTION TECHNIQUES IN *CAMERA WORK*

The complexity of the processes that form part of any investigations into photographic printing is nowhere more evident than in the work of the pictorialists. These photographers used, and sometimes invented, a whole variety of techniques designed to make artistic prints that would be produced in very small numbers, if not actually singly.

On the other hand, Stieglitz and his fellow Photo-Secessionists, in their concern to produce faithful copies of the works they wished to introduce to the public through the medium of *Camera Work*, always brought meticulous attention to bear on reproduction techniques (with which they were in any case intimately acquainted). The magazine delighted in providing a wide-ranging sample of such techniques.

1. Techniques for making original prints

The following three techniques are the simplest:
- **Gelatin silver print**. The most popular method at the turn of the century, frequently used by Stieglitz, Käsebier, and others.
- **Silver chloride print**. The paper, which was slow to respond to light, produced a subtle range of greys, and was particularly prized by Stieglitz for this reason.
- **Platinum print or platinotype**. Paper prepared using platinum salts became commercially available in around 1880 but disappeared after the 1914–18 war because of the prohibitive price of the metal. Besides ensuring the near-permanence of the print, this type of paper facilitated a delicate range in the mid-tone and shadow areas and was a favourite technique of White and de Meyer, among others. The resulting print has a matt appearance and tends towards silvery or (after toning) sepia tones.

More complicated techniques

- **Carbon print**. This process was developed by Alphonse Louis Poitevin in 1855 and perfected by Sir Joseph Wilson Swan in 1864. Thanks to the presence of the carbon, the print produced using this method is all but permanent – the chief merit of this particular process. Before being sensitized with potassium bichromate, the paper was coated with a mixture of gelatin and vegetable carbon powder, and then exposed to light under the negative. Since the resulting image was inverted, it had to be transferred on to a second plate by repeating the process. The carbon print generally has a velvety brown or black look to it.

- **Gum bichromate print**. This method dates back to the 19th century. Resurrected by Rouillé-Ladévèze and, first and foremost, by Robert Demachy, it became the favourite technique of the European and also of a number of American pictorialists, including Steichen. The paper was coated with a mixture of gum arabic, ground pigment and potassium bichromate, and then exposed under the negative. If two or more colours were required, the whole process could be repeated using two or three further coatings of gum bichromate (a method favoured by Steichen). The resulting print is coloured, grainy and sometimes uneven, and the running and scumbling of the pigment, together with the occasional brush stroke, creates a highly pictorial effect. Since the printing process altered to a greater or lesser degree the negative image (which was often enlarged), the original could be reproduced either from the print itself by the half-tone process or from the negative by photogravure, being then retouched by hand (Steichen's preferred method).

- **Gum platinum print**. In order either to add greater depth to their platinum prints, or to produce multiple prints from a single gum bichromate print, Coburn, and Steichen in particular, combined the platinum and gum bichromate processes. After first making a very light platinum print, the paper was then sensitized with gum bichromate and re-exposed under the same negative. Alternatively, a platinum print could be the counterpart to an original gum bichromate print.

• **Ozotype**. This was a combination of the carbon and gum bichromate methods. The ozotype was obtained by pressing a sheet of tissue coated with carbon into contact with a gum-sensitized print that had first been exposed under the negative. This obviated the double transfer necessitated by the carbon method used by itself and enabled the development of the image to be controlled.

• **Autochrome**. Developed between 1904 and 1907 by the Lumière brothers, this process, which produced a positive image directly between two glass plates, was the first commercially available colour process. It was used by Stieglitz, Steichen, Kuehn and others.

2. Reproduction processes

• **Photogravure**. This process was invented by Nicéphore Niepce and perfected by Fox Talbot and Niepce de Saint-Victor. It was used in *Camera Work* in the form perfected by Karl Klic in 1879. The process consists of exposing under the negative a metal plate coated in gelatin bichromate or bitumen and grained with resin powder. The resistance of the plate's surface to the corrosive effects of the acid depends on the intensity of light to which it is exposed and determines in turn the depth of the etching. Photogravure is the most faithful method of photographic reproduction, since the etched plate can retain a greater quantity of ink than the photo-lithographic plate or the half-tone, for example, and is better able to render the mid-tone and shadow areas. In *Camera Work*, the photogravures were often produced from the original negative and under the supervision of the photographer (details on these points are given in each issue of the magazine).

• **Hand-toned photogravure**. A number of Steichen's photographs were reproduced for *Camera Work* using this method.

• **Duogravure**. This process uses a double impression of the image, as a means either of adding colour or of deepening the tones.

• **Mezzotint photogravure**. This process aims at creating the effect of manual retouching (cf. Kuehn).

• **Half-tone**. Invented by Charles Petit in 1878 and perfected by George Meisenbach in 1882 and by Frederick Ives in 1886, this commercial reproduction method enables a photographic image to be integrated into printed type. The image is photographed through a mesh screen, which breaks it up into minute, variously sized dots to create areas of light, shade and intermediate tones. *Camera Work* was not initially concerned with printing images and text simultaneously, since, with the exception of the ornamental letters, all its illustrations were produced independently of the text. Half-tones were eventually introduced into the magazine, probably partly with the aim of exploring a new technique, and also no doubt for economic reasons. The half-tone process is cruder and less faithful to the original than photogravure, but also less costly. It is sometimes effective, nevertheless, in rendering highly contrasty images.

Camera Work contains a total of 559 plates, of which 126 are half-tones, 409 photogravures and 4 duogravures.

BIOGRAPHIES OF THE PRINCIPAL *CAMERA WORK* PHOTOGRAPHERS

Bold figures in brackets refer to plate nos.

James Craig Annan (1864–1946).

He trained with his father, Thomas Annan, a professional photographer based in Glasgow. Craig Annan joined the group the Linked Ring in 1894 and became the principal representative of pictorialism in Scotland, exhibiting works at the Photo-Club de Paris and the Photo-Secession gallery in New York. He was one of the first exponents of photogravure, a technique he learnt from Karl Klic in Vienna, and his first attempts in this field in 1890 were directed at reproducing his father's works, as also works by Hill and Adamson. His own photographs combine realism with a strongly pictorial quality and are frequently reminiscent of painting (**32**).

Julia Margaret Cameron (1815–1879).

Born into a wealthy, cultured family, she came to photography as an amateur at the age of fifty. Her timeless portraits of important figures from the social circles in which she moved completely transformed the aesthetic upon which the photographic portrait had been based. Cameron was always popular in Great Britain and the pictorialists particularly admired her use of soft focus, hailing her as one of the precursors of their movement. She was a precursor also in the sense that she introduced fiction into photography by illustrating the poems of Tennyson (**36**).

Alvin Langdon Coburn (1882–1966).

A photographer of precocious talent, he was encouraged in his endeavours by Frederick Holland Day. In 1902, Coburn opened a studio in New York, where he got to know Stieglitz, worked with Käsebier, and was elected an associate member of the Photo-Secession. Coburn's best work dates from around 1912, during the period when he was working in England and distancing himself from pictorialism. *Clouds* (1912), one of the many books he illustrated, marks one of the high points of his art and reflects his leanings towards mysticism and abstraction (**13, 29, 34, 38**).

Robert Demachy (1859–1936).

The son of a banker, Demachy developed an interest in photography in around 1880 and became one of the leading figures of European pictorialism. In 1894, he co-founded the Photo-Club de Paris and organized its first show at the Galerie Durand-Ruel. He resurrected the gum bichromate printing method, which he passed on to the European and American pictorialists, subsequently perfecting various other techniques derived from this one, such as the oil-pigment process and the oil-transfer process. Demachy was on very good terms with Stieglitz and it was he who selected the photographs for the French pictorialist exhibitions held in New York and London. During the 1914–1918 war he abandoned photography for drawing (**12, 16, 17, 24, 31**).

Frank Eugene (1865–1936).

A painter who had undergone his training at the Academy of Fine Arts in Munich, he began practising photography as an amateur in 1883 and co-founded the Photo-Secession group in 1902. In 1906, he settled in Germany for good, intending to pursue his career as a painter, but finally opted to practise and teach pictorialist photography, a field in which he was enormously successful, since a chair of pictorial photography was specially created for him at the Academy of Fine Arts in Leipzig (**23, 42**).

Frederick Henry Evans (1853–1943).

A bookseller, friend of the illustrator Aubrey Beardsley and the writer George Bernard Shaw, in 1898 Evans decided to devote himself full-time to photography following an initial introduction to it via microphotography in 1880. He continued to practise photography until 1912, joined the Linked Ring, entered into a correspondence with Stieglitz in 1901, and in 1906 exhibited at Gallery 291, the Photo-Secessionists' gallery in New York. The reproductions of his works in *Camera Work* do not do full justice to his platinum prints (his favourite printing technique). His impressive, highly disciplined oeuvre primarily comprises views of buildings, woods and a small number of portraits; of all the pictorialists, Evans was the most original (**27**).

Paul Haviland (1880–1950).

Haviland's father was the owner of the famous Haviland porcelain works in Limoges, and it was on a business trip to New York in 1908 on behalf of his father's company that Haviland met Stieglitz. He immediately began playing an energetic role in the activities of the Photo-Secession magazine and gallery, which he supported financially. In 1915 Haviland co-founded the review *291* with various other avant-garde members of the group.

David Octavius Hill (1802–1870).

A painter of mediocre talent, member of Edinburgh's Royal Academy, Hill used photography to help him carry out his more ambitious projects on canvas. In his pre-1850 photographic portraits of Edinburgh's clerical society figures and of Newhaven fishermen, he maximized the aesthetic potential offered by the simplifications inherent in the calotype method, developed by Fox Talbot in 1839. Craig Annan introduced his work to the pictorialists, for whom he became a model. The important role played by Robert Adamson (who died in 1848) as Hill's technical collaborator was not recognized until much later (**26, 28**).

Theodor Hofmeister (1863 or 1865–1943) and Oscar Hofmeister (1869 or 1871–1937).

Theodor was a wholesaler and Oscar a town clerk in Hamburg. In 1895, the two brothers began practising amateur photography and became a part of Hamburg's photographic community. They always worked together, Theodor taking the photographs and Oscar printing them using the gum bichromate method, which he had learnt from

Kuehn. Their favourite subject was landscape, into which human figures were sometimes incorporated, these figures being treated sometimes in a realistic manner (scenes of country folk) or, as in *The Solitary Horseman*, in a romantic spirit. In around 1910, the Hofmeister brothers switched from gum bichromate to contact printing (**22**).

Frederick Holland Day (1864–1933).

Day played an active role in the development of pictorialism, but always maintained his independence as an artist.

Alfred Horsley Hinton (1863–1908).

After receiving an artistic training, he headed a firm producing photographic materials and, in the process, developed a passion for photography. He edited the *Photographic Journal* from 1887 to 1891, opened a portrait studio in Guildford, conceived and co-founded the group the Linked Ring, and from 1893 until his death contributed to the review *The Amateur Photographer*. His contemporaries viewed him as one of the founders of English landscape photography, but his work is widely scattered today, and continues to be little known. He avoided manipulation during the printing process but was not averse to retouching his negatives, which were themselves assembled from more than one original (**19**).

Gertrude Käsebier (1852–1934).

Käsebier came from a fairly humble background, but her strong personality helped her to make her mark. She studied painting in Brooklyn and turned to photography in around 1892. She continued to develop her technique in Europe, then, in 1897, opened a portrait studio in New York. Attention was drawn to her work at the Philadelphia Salon of 1889. She joined New York's Camera Club, and in 1902 co-founded the Photo-Secession group, which she left in 1912, later co-founding the American Pictorialists with Clarence White. Her work, which was much admired by contemporaries, mainly comprises portraits and mother-and-child studies (**49**).

Heinrich Kuehn (1866–1944).

Kuehn joined Vienna's Camera-Club in 1896, exhibited work alongside Munich's Secessionist artists in 1898, and founded the Trifolium with two fellow Austrian photographers. He met Stieglitz in 1904 and was subsequently influenced by the American pictorialists, transforming his style and lightening his technique (to include the gum bichromate, oil-pigment and transfer processes) so that it became more strictly photographic. While the movement was in general decline, Kuehn himself succeeded up until about 1930 in producing a belated but highly personal, full-blown version of pictorialism. Most notable are his nude studies, landscapes and still lifes, which are printed in several colours and display remarkable technical skill (**7, 30**).

René Le Bègue.

Though, like them, a founder-member of the Photo-Club de Paris in 1894, Le Bègue played a less active role than either Puyo or Demachy in defending pictorialism in France. As a result, little is known about either his personality or the details of his life. Le Bègue nevertheless left a quite remarkable oeuvre, exclusively composed, it seems, of gum bichromate prints of female nudes in deep shades of black, blue and orange-red. His figures, with their blurred outlines, frequently draped and set against an abstract background, are reminiscent of the best academic tradition. Le Bègue was not seeking to interpret modern life by drawing his inspiration from the subject matter and composition of the Impressionist painters – which was Demachy's forte – but, like the Impressionists, he worked in the open air.

Adolf de Meyer (1868–1946).

De Meyer was born in Dresden. In 1893 he was exhibiting his photographs in London and in Paris, where they came to Stieglitz's attention. Two years later, de Meyer moved to London and married Olga Carraciolo, the illegitimate daughter of the Prince of Wales. The cosmopolitan, high-society life-style he enjoyed in London did nothing to detract from his work as a photographer – quite the contrary. The 1912 issue of *Camera Work* devoted to him demonstrates the extreme modernism inherent in his rejection of manipulative techniques and of pictorialist sentimentalism. He likewise harnessed his taste for fiction and his inventiveness in the creation of a new genre: fashion photography. He and Steichen were the first photographers to work for magazines like *Vogue* and *Harper's Bazaar* (from 1914). De Meyer ended his days in relative poverty and artistic obscurity (**8, 33, 43, 44**).

Emile Joachim Constant Puyo (1857–1933).

A military man, Puyo began taking amateur photographs in about 1889. He was very close to Demachy and in 1894 joined the Photo-Club de Paris, which he helped Demachy run. Together, they experimented with printing processes such as gum bichromate and oil-pigment. A recent exhibition brought to light a vein of his photographic work that Puyo kept under wraps in his own lifetime (and which is all the more

interesting for that): direct prints that have not been subjected to manipulation. In 1914, Puyo returned to soldiering but did not give up photography, and he continued to publish his writings on the subject (**52**).

George Henry Seeley (1880–1955).

Seeley spent his whole life in the environs of Boston, where his father worked as an estate manager. He studied art and design, and in 1902, under the influence of Frederick Holland Day, he took up photography again, having first practised it as a child. After a first one-man show in Stockbridge and a show in New York, Stieglitz asked Seeley to join the Photo-Secession. Like White, Seeley was drawn to mysterious and intimate scenes, and fascinated by the play of light, particularly reflected light, a theme dear to the pictorialists in general. An exhibition in Buffalo in 1910 showed a collection of quasi-abstract compositions by Seeley – gum bichromate prints of snowy landscapes. By 1920, he had more or less given up photography in favour of painting and ornithology (**41**).

Edward Steichen (1894–1973).

Steichen came from a humble family who had settled in Milwaukee in 1881. He studied art and his work attracted notice at the Philadelphia photographic salon of 1899. Through Clarence White, Steichen got to know Stieglitz. His frequent visits to Europe from 1900 onwards and his familiarity with the avant-garde European artistic milieu placed him in the role of an artistic adviser to his fellow Photo-Secessionists. During the war his experience of aerial photography renewed Steichen's links with photography in general and from now on he devoted himself exclusively to this medium. He was appointed director of the Department of Photography at New York's Museum of Modern Art in 1947, and was responsible for organizing the famous 'Family of Man' exhibition; but well before this appointment he had been working to ensure the spread of photography both in artistic circles and among the public at large. Steichen was one of the great masters of pictorialism, but pictorialism represented only one aspect of his work, which was almost as rich and multifarious in its development as Stieglitz's (**1, 2, 3, 4, 6, 11, 14, 15, 18, 23, 35, 37, 39, 45, 47, 54**).

Alfred Stieglitz (1864–1946).

The son of a wealthy industrialist, Stieglitz was educated in Europe, where he first began practising photography. By the time he returned to the United States in 1890, his resolve was firmly set on moulding the future course of artistic photography in his homeland. The most influential member of the Club for American Amateur Photographers and of New York's Camera Club, whose magazines he edited, in 1902 he created his own group, the Photo-Secession, and in 1903 the magazine *Camera Work*, thanks to which he became a prominent member of the American cultural avant-garde. In 1917, he decided to devote himself full-time to photography, a course he followed for the next twenty years. In the mean while, he also found time to open two new galleries in New York: The Intimate Gallery (1925) and An American Place (1929). Pictorialism was no more than an episode in the career of this photographer – one of the greatest of all modern photographers – and the best of his work dates, in fact, from after 1915 (**46, 50, 51, 53, 55, 56, 57, 58**).

Paul Strand (1890–1976).

Strand studied photography under Lewis Hine, who introduced him to Gallery 291. Stieglitz recognized in him one of the great photographers of the 20th century and devoted the last two issues of *Camera Work* (in 1916 and 1917) to his work, which was by now already beginning to turn its back on the pictorialist aesthetic. In 1932, after a stint working as a cameraman, Strand was asked by the Mexican government to run the department of film and photography at the Museum of Fine Arts. He travelled extensively – in Egypt, the USSR, Italy and France – and a section of his work reflects his interest in the political and social realities that were a far cry from pictorialist concerns (**59, 60, 61**).

Clarence Hudson White (1871–1925).

Thanks to straitened family circumstances, White was prevented from following his inclination and taking up artistic studies. From 1893 he practised photography part-time, while continuing to work for a living. In 1898, he founded the Camera Club of Newark and in 1899 Stieglitz devoted an exhibition to his work in New York. A founder-member of the Photo-Secession in 1902, White finally broke with Stieglitz in 1912. Thanks to his temperament and poetic gifts, White was one of the most inspired of all the pictorialists. From 1914, he spent most of his time teaching photography, opening a school in Maine, and later one in New York (**5, 9, 20, 40**).

BIBLIOGRAPHY

The anastatic reprint of *Camera Work* in 1969 by Kraus, Liechtenstein, enables the reader to familiarize him- or herself with the critical texts and format of the magazine, but utterly sacrifices the quality of the original illustrations.

The sumptuous work by Jonathan Green, *Camera Work: A Critical Anthology*, 1973 (Aperture, New York) provides only a selection of texts and illustrations but does full justice to the elegance and style of the magazine's presentation and the quality of its reproductions. The anthology is supplemented with a historical and critical overview, a list of all the published issues of the magazine, together with notes on the photographers, artists and writers who collaborated on it or appear within its pages, and an exhaustive bibliography.

A less ambitious work, Marianne Fulton Margolis's *Camera Work: A Pictorial Guide*, 1978 (Dover, New York, and Constable, London) nevertheless has the advantage of reproducing in chronological order the magazine's 559 plates (that is, the entirety of its illustrations barring advertising material), together with a brief historical overview, detailed and valuable notes on technical processes and an index of artists' names and titles of works.

Among the many works devoted to pictorialism and looking beyond the confines of the magazine *Camera Work*, one worth noting is Robert Doty's *Photo Secession: Photography as a Fine Art*, 1960 (George Eastman House, Rochester). The first work on the subject, now a classic, it reproduces illustrations (of which it has 56 in all) from both *Camera Work* and the second magazine Stieglitz edited, *Camera Notes*.

The Collection of Alfred Stieglitz, 1978 (Metropolitan Museum and Viking Press, New York), the extensive catalogue of the exhibition of the same title, with texts by Weston Naef, assisted by the pupils of the William Homer School, provides a very detailed account of the creation of the Photo-Secessionist movement and of the magazine *Camera Work*. Above all, it offers a sort of illustrated dictionary of the principal American and European pictorialist photographers whose works were collected by Stieglitz (and, thanks to him, are housed today in New York's Metropolitan Museum).

The study by Margaret Harker, *The Linked Ring (1892–1910)*, 1979 (Heinemann, London), whose remarkable historical introduction is accompanied by carefully selected illustrations and biographical notes on the photographers, places the Photo-Secession movement (whose principal members also belonged to the Linked Ring) within the context of European pictorialism.

PHOTOFILE

Titles in this series include:
American Photographers of the Depression
Eugène Atget
Werner Bischof
The Origins of British Photography
Brassaï
Camera Work
Robert Capa
Henri Cartier-Bresson
Bruce Davidson
Robert Doisneau
Robert Frank
André Kertész
Jacques-Henri Lartigue
Photomontage
Marc Riboud
Man Ray
Duane Michals
Helmut Newton
The Nude
W. Eugene Smith
Weegee

The Photofile series is conceived and produced
by the Centre National de la Photographie, Paris,
under the direction of Robert Delpire.